Letters to a Student

Staying close to Christ during the university years

Dear Neil,

I hope you enjoy getting to know my dear friend and Mentor, Donald through these letters.

Ben

Donald Drew has drawn on his wide experience of the student world in writing these imaginary letters to a Christian young man going up to university for the first time. He has an unerring touch and strikes all the right notes. There is not a trace of paternalism, just a warm, humorous epistolary style spiced with wisdom and affection. I found it irresistible reading and was sorry when it came to an end. Any young person receiving such a book would be sure to find it wholly beneficial and spiritually reassuring. I hope that many will find themselves indebted to Drew through being given this book before a new academic year begins.

Bishop John B. Taylor, Cambridge

I hope this book becomes available across the country because it can only be good for students following Jesus to be encouraged and challenged in so many areas of life – it really does read easily and enjoyably.

Nick Houston, Student

Having known some of the great Christian leaders of the last century, Donald Drew combines, as they did, truth and grace. His book of letters is supremely practical even though it is designed for the university student, its counsel applies to every age. He candidly expounds what he knows intimately and humbly points to many other authors, poets and theologians. His words are uniquely compelling because he is so informed on the past and knows the precise lessons from history inform the present. Throughout a wide diversity of practical topics he writes like an affectionate uncle and peer. At the same time Dr Drew shows how he rests in God and encourages readers to do the same. Very readable!

Dr Art Lindsley, Senior Fellow,
CS Lewis Institute, Virgina
Fourth Presbyterian Church in Metropolitan
Washington, DC

These letters represent the distilled wisdom of a lifetime spent befriending and advising young people. They are full of practical and reliable help across a wide range of concerns. The author's insights about the culture in which students live today makes them worthwhile for that alone. But he aims for Christian integrity of life as well as thought and so has plenty of challenges about lifestyle and attitudes. But he does this without ever being simplistic or legalistic. In fact the letters radiate an atmosphere of cultured humanity, kindness, hope and respect – which is just what is needed today.

Ranald Macaulay, Cambridge

Dr Drew reminds us in his unusual and highly readable book, *Letters to a Student*, that mentoring is critically important to the shaping of young lives. He lovingly and candidly engages the range of issues facing students today, yet does so in a non-sanctimonious fashion. He embraces the total person in all of the complexity and wonder inherent in being human. He is comfortable with the range of experiences and emotions, sadness and joy, fear and hope. In that sense, he is calling his young charge to bring all that he is and does to his Lord. There is no false dichotomy drawn between the 'secular' and 'spiritual'. His challenge to a young person is simple and profound: decisions make a difference. Each one has a consequence. Dr Drew has done us a great service in showing that followership must at its heart be brutally honest and real, lived out in the context of relationship.

Ambassador J. Douglas Holladay, Washington, DC

Every Christian student ought to have older, wiser friends who know God well and have a lot of Christian life experience behind them. I wish I had known Dr Drew when I was a student. In this collection of letters to a student, Dr Drew draws on long experience of being a student, an encourager of students and a Christian apologist to provide clear, warm advice on standing firm for Christ during college years. From worldviews to sex, from guidance to friendship and from prayer to pursuing academic excellence, each short letter is punchy, well informed and readable. Any student would benefit from having this wide-ranging, enjoyable book on their shelf.

Marcus Honeysett, UCCF Teamleader in London

Letters to a Student is a book that encapsulates the essence of Donald Drew and his strong Christian beliefs. In the collected writings what consistently shines through is his humanity, an overwhelming sense of spiritual guidance and an inexhaustible supply of sound common sense based on a lifetime's experience of thoughtful consideration for others.

It is populated with insightful anecdotes, references and interesting stories that cause one to pause and reflect, sometimes from a humorous standpoint but more frequently to consider the often-profound observations about university, society and indeed life in general. I would recommend its inclusion in a survival kit for all prospective university students.

Sir John Stevens QPM DL,
Former Commissioner for the Metropolitan Police,
London

Having had two children too, and through, university and with two more children to progress on beyond school, the immense value of Dr Drew's 'Letters to a Student' strikes me very personally. I also had the first hand value of his wisdom as one of my mentors when I was a schoolboy. The style of his book is crisp, direct and cuts straight to the core of so many key spiritual issues, yet it does so in a delightfully human and sympathetic way. By adopting a letter form, it is instantly personal and naturally allows the subject matter to be dealt with in easily digestible portiona. And it is the subject matter which is so compelling – wise comment from the perspective or mature experience founded on biblical truths – which makes this book invaluable for responsible parents and apprehensive potential students alike.

Lt- Gen. F R Dannatt,
Allied Command Europe Rapid Reaction Corps

Being taken through the three years of a student's university experience with all the issues, thoughts and problems that come with that, as well as being taught so much in terms of biblical truths, personal reflections, contemporary student problems, Christian unions and prayer, was really helpful.

Katherine Cooper, student

Letters to a Student

Staying close to Christ
during the university years

Letters from an older friend to a student friend

DONALD J DREW

CHRISTIAN FOCUS

SOLI DEO GLORIA

To the memory of my parents, teachers and mentors

past and present

and

to students who are wanting purpose and meaning

in their lives.

ISBN 1-85792-866-0

© Copyright Donald J Drew 2003

Published in 2003
Reprinted 2005
by
Christian Focus Publications, Ltd.
Geanies House, Fearn, Tain,
Ross-shire, IV20 ITW, Great Britain.

www.christianfocus.com

Printed and bound by
Norhaven Paperback A/S, Denmark

Cover Design by Alister MacInnes

CONTENTS

Foreword 9
Preface 13

On Going to University 15
Your First Two Weeks 19
University Christian Unions 22
A Brief Note 26
Mentoring and Self-Discipline 27
Today's Controlling Ideas 32
Getting Alongside Students 35
Two Conflicting World-Views 39
Presenting the Christian Position 41
Confirming the Christian Position 43
Postmodernism 45
The Bible's Framework 48
Your Most Precious Possession 53
Always your Most Precious Possession 59
A Postcript 63
A Unique Privilege 64
Always a Unique Privilege 69
Keeping the Lines Open 74
Faith 79
Doubt 84
Frailty & Foolishness: The Tables Turned 87
Temptation 89
Another Brief Note 93
Guidance 95
Uncovering your Gifts 99
Deeds not Words 102
Friendship and Hardship 108
Why Bother? 112

A Great Example 115
A Great Resource 119
Christian Books and Bookshops 124
Why Bother With Literature? 127
Some Questions to be asked of Lecturers 131
Some Questions to be asked of
Films, Books and Television 137
Forgetting to Remember: Reconsidering History 140
Forgetting to Remember: The Loss of a Christian Memory: ... 143
Christianity is Universal Truth 146
A Further Brief Note 150
The Consuming Culture of Consumerism 151
Wedlock of Deadlock? 158
Marriage or Singleness? 163
The Day of Reckoning! 168
My Story 169
Alpine Mountaineering 173
The Drag and Delight of Daily Labour 178
What Next? 183
Anticipating the Future 184
On Leaving University 187
Books Mentioned in Order of the Letters 190

FOREWORD

Every young Christian should have a Donald Drew in his or her life – a wise, older Christian friend whose encouragement, counsel, and care are an invaluable guide through the crucial early years of life. Obviously we all have our families. In most parts of the world we also have school teachers and many of us have also had influential figures such as ministers, sports coaches, music teachers and university tutors to whom we owe so much in different ways. But for me and many others I know, the place of an older Christian friend outside these other roles has been decisive and irreplaceable. Donald Drew has been just that in my life and in the life of an extraordinary number of others I know and *Letters to a Student* gives an idea why.

I first met him when I was twelve and a shy new boy in the school where he both taught English and was the Housemaster of the house that was the main rival to my own. Since I was in a different house and he taught only the upper forms, I knew him only from a distance during my first years at the school.

All that changed when he became my teacher in the sixth form and English became my favourite subject. Looking back, I am amazed at the profound influence Donald had in my life, both then and since. It is quite simply true to say that he inspired in me a life-long love for words, for the beauty and clarity of the English language, for the deep humanity and brilliance of William Shakespeare, for the robust traditions of the English stage, for the importance of enjoying the classics long after school days are over – and most importantly of all for me – an appreciation and love of writing and public speaking. And all this in the context of his clear and attractive faith in God.

I have written or edited more than twenty books today, but I had absolutely no thoughts of being a writer when I was growing up. It was he who suggested the idea of my first book to me, almost accidentally and many years after leaving school. He is also responsible for my start in public speaking, though in that case his influence was more deliberate.

All the way through school I was far too shy to think of speaking in public, and though there are remarkable orators in our family history, I had no idea of it then and my parents had given me no encouragement in that direction. He, however, helped put me forward for my first debate – to propose the motion that "This house regrets the Russian revolution." The correctness of that argument was far less evident then than it is today, and my opponent was the champion debater in the school. So doubtless I over-prepared and I could have given the speech word for word ten years later. But what sealed the evening as a milestone moment in my life was not winning the debate; it was the little four-word note that he passed to me as I sat down, signed with the characteristic flourish of his initials – "DJD". That thoughtful note was such an encouragement and inspiration to me that I made a commitment that night to take as many opportunities as I could to learn the art of public speaking.

Many years have come and gone since that evening in my final year at school, and Donald Drew has been a constant part of many of them – first in England, then at the L'Abri community in Switzerland, and most recently in the United States where his annual visits are eagerly anticipated by an astonishing number of people of all ages who find in him a wisdom and encouragement that is as rare as the finest gold. Much is said about "mentors" these days, and much of it flatters only to deceive. But Donald is the real thing. He is a born teacher, an unashamed lover of ideas and of English, a connoisseur of beautiful music, a veteran walker and great mountain climber and a passionate lover of the Matterhorn in all its splendour and many moods.

But that barely begins to describe the man. Far deeper still, he is a magnificent friend and an older brother in the faith whose character and experience of God are the result of years of walking with Christ, whose wisdom comes from his own learning from the great saints of his lifetime and the giants before them, whose love is generous and constant, whose counsel is unerring, whose prayers and notes of encouragement are legendary, and whose fun and youthful spirit is as fresh as the day when each of us who are his friends first met him.

Do you have an older brother or sister in the faith to be your constant friend and ever-available counsellor? Do you have someone in your life to encourage the cultivation of your gifts, someone who will be there when you hit a spot of trouble, and whom you know is always thinking and praying about your best? Sadly, there are not enough Donald Drews in the Christian community today.

These *Letters to a Student* obviously lack the unique warmth, the inimitable touches and unforgettable idiosyncracies, of the real man who is behind them. But they come with the wisdom, care and encouragement that we his friends appreciate so much, and that we all need as we in our turn seek to follow Christ in this crazy old world today.

Os Guinness

PREFACE

These letters derive a great deal from working with students over many years and in particular from two older friends and their wives, Bob Kramer who suggested the idea and Os Guinness who endorsed it. My grateful thanks are due to them and other friends including John Barrs, Timothy Blake, Ben Griffiths, Doug and Ann Holladay, Ryan Holladay and Becca Newell, Katherine Cooper and Nicholas Houston, all of whom read the manuscript and urged me towards the printing press. I am indebted also to David Porter who painstakingly scrutinised these Letters and to Mary Byham who turned many hieroglyphics into a readable manuscript. All these folk may take some credit for the 'perfections'. The imperfections are mine.

I would like to express my thanks to Anne Norrie, my Editor, for unstinted helpfulness and to the staff of Christian Focus Publications.

My sincere thanks are due also to those busy friends who kindly and willingly endorsed this book and to another busy friend, Os Guinness, for his generous and affectionate Foreword.

Should I have failed to acknowledge the source of a quotation, an insight or turn of phrase, my apologies are due for that was not intentional. As for omissions, I plead as did Dr Johnson: 'Ignorance madam, pure ignorance.'

D.J.D

NOTE: All author royalities from the sale of this book will go to encourage HELP A CHILD (established 68 years ago) which gives financial support to Christian partner organizations in several countries in Asia and Africa. The support is for helping children in need who, in children's homes, receive love, care, food and education and hear the gospel of Christ.

ON GOING TO UNIVERSITY

Dear Richard,

So you go to university next Friday. Congratulations and celebrations! I am pleased to know that it is the one of your first choice. During your progress from toddler to teenager there have been several rites of passage, stepping-stones with a wider gap between them each time, that have led you onward. An increasing number of your contemporaries, for various reasons, are hoping to enter one of our many universities or colleges. My generation went, believe it or not, to one of only 17 universities to enjoy what such institutions alone can give. There are now 84 classified universities in the United Kingdom.

We thought it not a right but a privilege, something special. So it is and I loved it. We went to university because we wanted to learn and learn how to learn. Your having had a Gap Year will, I think, increase eagerness to study because from a small boy, you've never been a sluggard!

The student world has always been an exciting place, crammed with people of all sorts and activities of all kinds. The poet William Wordsworth's expression of his early admiration for the French Revolution can be applied to many students' feelings at having been at university or college: "Bliss was it in that dawn to be alive, but to be young was very heaven!" It is a unique, once-in-a-lifetime experience comprising all manner of valuable and valid experiences, as you will be aware from having perused the *Alternative Prospectus*! And you will be unlikely to have such unusual freedom again. Most of the thousands of students entering university will not have enjoyed such independence before, nor experienced such a variety of societies and clubs and sports.

With such exciting options open to you, I hope you are ready unashamedly to speak up and tell other Freshers that you are a Christian, and they will be impressed if they know that you have also signed up for one or two other societies and clubs!

From now on there will be no more roll-calls, no being home at a certain time, no getting up at a certain time – a free-for-all and for many students, perhaps most, it's their idea of paradise! But reality will sweep in: tutors set essays, lecturers require your attendance, bills have to be paid.

Yet there is another side. Many people who know what they are talking about would say that much of the contemporary university culture is rotten at its core, a statement that includes curriculum, teaching and morality. Campuses have been likened to brothels where sex of various kinds is widely and uninhibitedly available. Mercilessly driven by the media, the urgency for teenagers and young adults to have earlier and earlier sex has no parallel in British history. It is even assumed that if a teenager has not had sex, there must be something wrong with him or her. A chorus of increasingly deregulated TV, the Internet, DVDs, cinema, pop music and teen magazines unite in singing of sex as the apogee of being a young adult, even though for some it may be an attempt to find a denied love and some meaning for their lives.

As for religious beliefs in general, anything goes: pick 'n' mix from a spiritual supermarket. The chameleon-like word 'spirituality' covers any way of making a person feel better, such as pop psychology, closeness to nature, the occult, astrology and especially New Age ideas. There's plenty of "spiritual awareness" (whatever that may mean) but little if any, spiritual alertness, discernment. It's an area where no assumptions are made, no questions are asked. This makes it easier for you initially to be accepted as a follower of Jesus Christ but you'll soon be asked to justify your convictions. In addition to Christian or religious societies, there will be a number of other 'faith communities' who guard their members and are intolerant of others' beliefs.

You will find many students who, despite appearances, have a deep-seated sense of meaninglessness and hopelessness. They may have come from homes in which there are often few books or interesting conversations. Even more come from scarred or unloving, crumbling or crashed families and bring hurts and harms with them. Most of them will have to confront at close quarters issues of personal identity and their emphasis is likely to be self-expressive rather than accepting responsibility for themselves. Debt, the pressure of part-time jobs, loneliness, having to deal with a backlog of reading because of years of gazing at TV; each of these will need some putting right. And there will alas! be a number of folk who realise they ought not to be at university at all. These and other pressure-points contribute to suicide being now, after accidents, the second most common cause of death for young people between the ages of 15 and 24.

Students, provided they have really sorted out why they are at university, should be alright as long as they resolve to live sensibly, find reliable friends and do not lose sight of their priorities. These same requirements apply to you. At first, you may feel lonely and even homesick. But when you remember that each Fresher is thinking similar thoughts and feeling similar things, look forward to what is ahead and go for it! Self-awareness and strangeness should swiftly pass. Smile at the next student you meet and the one after that which will help to remove the strangeness and to settle you!

As a follower of Jesus Christ, you will have potential friends in the Christian Union. Each of you Christian Freshers needs to identify with the Christians already there, in order for you to be seen to be a body making an impression on the student body. Right from the start, nail your colours to the mast. On arrival, find where the CU meets and get stuck into it and you'll find like-minded people who need you as you need them. Also find friends elsewhere. When one's years at university or college are over, one wants to be able to look back on them as a time when, among other things, some wholesome friendships were formed and contact was made with some fine men and women who gained one's respect and affection, when, as Os Guinness said, "the blood ran fast and the mind ran deep".

You are at university in the Midlands and student life in Britain is varied. For example, some things will apply at vocational training colleges that do not apply at a university. In the same way, not all CUs are run on the same pattern. I am glad to know that you have already found a church. Some churches seem unsatisfactory and not to everyone's taste. If I were in your shoes, I'd want a Bible-based, Christ-centred, caring community where I was among folk who were as "afraid, difficult, damaged and sinful as I was", which, if it disappeared tomorrow, I'd desperately miss. I hope you find that yours is one of these, a church whose members arouse people's curiosity. You students in the CU need a church to remind you of the larger world and to feed you spiritually, while you need the CU individually and collectively to remind the university that the God who is there is the only God who is there.

In conclusion, may I gently and firmly remind you that you are not at university primarily to evangelize your contemporaries! You are there to get the best degree you can. You gained entry principally on account of your academic achievements and anticipated attainments, not because you are a follower of the Lord Jesus Christ. To you, much has been given. From you, much will be required. Get naturally alongside your contemporaries, regarding them as real human beings made in the image of God, to be loved not for what they project, but for themselves. They're not 'gospel fodder' as some kinds of evangelism might imply. Be friendly to all who cross your path, find godly, fun-loving believers and keep your priorities a priority, top of the list being what you told me some weeks ago, that you are going to show whose side you are on.

All good wishes

Donald

PS. Did you know that you are one of 1,859,600 enrolments in the various higher education institutions in the U.K. during the academic year 2001-2002!

YOUR FIRST TWO WEEKS

Dear Richard,

Thank you for your letter and I'm relieved to know that mine gave you a reasonably realistic entry into aspects of university life, which was its intention. But it's no surprise that you're already struggling with some concerns. Invariably today, and it was much the same in my day, these seemingly revolve round lifestyle and relationships. Lifestyle especially is the issue. It's not an issue for others because what is in fact often sin, they think of as a lifestyle. For you, it is a challenge you can take up and win, and often provides situations where discussions develop about the big questions.

As a believer you may now have to ask yourself some more questions about lifestyles and come up with the Christian answer, for example, today's attitude to sleeping around, or having a steady bed-partner, to homosexuality, to alcohol and drugs, to obeying the law, telling the truth, to freedom to express your faith. In a word, how are you to engage with these issues and not lose Christian distinctives? My hope is that my writing and our talking together will help a little to stimulate and embolden you.

As you doubtless know, being different from your contemporaries is a fate worse than death! It's the ultimate social sin. You can afford to be, and you will be anyway, different from your parents. But to be different from your peers! Jesus warned us that being ostracised, avoided by others, will happen to believers by those who do not know or who do not want to know, God. In the West, the Christian faith is being assaulted to the extent that in many parts of the world, it is fighting for its life. Multi-cultural and politically correct beliefs are uppermost in society and intolerant of opposition. The faith is under siege. But historically it has always been like that! Today's conditions are no worse than those that faced our first Christian brothers and sisters. You and I counter opposition and misunderstanding by an attractive, bold, articulate and holy lifestyle with a clear inner conviction that we are willing, if need be, to die for Christ as millions of our Christian brothers and sisters have done and are daily doing as I write and you read this.

You say that the student next door says that he drinks between six and eight pints a night. You frequently put him to bed and clean up the vomit. I too had to do that once or twice and what prompted me as a believer was that deeds speak louder than words. As has been said, 'people won't care how much you know until they know how much you care.' Be a good Samaritan to him. Put yourself in his place, both as to the mess and later thinking about your actions. You have a choice: either to love your neighbour as yourself or turn over and go to sleep. Loving others more than ourselves is risky, inconvenient, sacrificial. Jesus' story of the good Samaritan stings.

But think what can follow from this, Richard: the forming of a 'relationship' (for which every student is desperate), the beginning of a friendship which may take a couple of terms or a year. I think that his behaviour will have modified and at some point you'll find yourselves talking together about reality and truth. But had you told him to stew in his own juice and condemned him, a Berlin Wall would have gone up. I'm sure that there are more struggles ahead – and I do not mean necessarily with the student next door. I am sure also of one thing: you will have grown in true spirituality and be closer in your walk with God.

Keep on praying for him and for others around you. Ask the Lord to help you to be sure why your convictions about needing to be different are absolutely right. When you're assured of this, you won't need to worry about being courageous. A godly life, warmed by your humanness, will stand out. You'll feel easy about going out with some Freshers and unafraid to say 'No' to others. Spending time with them may not be the same as talking with them and disagreeing with them. There will be a good many times when you feel you're in a corner. But summon up that "lonely virtue" of courage. Be willing to be thought stupid or intolerant but knowing that because you kept on making points and trying to answer theirs in a pleasant way, you have gained their respect. That is a spring-board for the next time. Student conversations are not entirely about bikes, babes, booze and sex! And wherever you as a believer go, you are not only a presence; you are an influence. Remember that.

There is the story, often repeated, of the young police officer who was taking his final exam at Hendon Police College in north London. Here is one of the questions: 'You are on patrol in outer London when an explosion occurs in a gas main in a nearby street. On investigation, you find that a large hole has been blown in the footpath and there is an overturned van lying nearby. Inside the van there is a strong smell of alcohol. Both occupants, a man and a woman, are injured. You recognise the woman as the wife of your Divisional Inspector who is at present away in the USA. Suddenly a man runs out of a nearby house shouting that his wife is expecting a baby and that the shock of the explosion has made the birth imminent. Another man is crying for help, having been blown into an adjacent canal by the explosion and he cannot swim. Bearing in mind the provisions of the Mental Health Act, describe in a few words what action you would take.' The officer thought for a moment, picked up his pen and wrote: 'I would take off my uniform and mingle with the crowd.'

Each of us has to make a choice and then has to live with the consequences of that choice.

Thank you for telling me of your experiences. You know that I'm alongside you.

All good wishes

Donald

PS. After finals, Third years often sell some of their study books. If you're looking for such books, try the Students' Union bookshop first then the second-hand bookshops. But be quick off the mark!

UNIVERSITY CHRISTIAN UNIONS

Dear Richard,

Thinking back to my first letter, I was arrested by the fact that unlike my generation which was the first to have full financial grants, you will incur considerable debt on account of university fees. It's necessary fairly quickly to manage your budget, allocating money for books, meals, recreation, etc. And try to avoid falling into the trap of buying now and paying later. Don't spend money you haven't got. Remember: Credit = Debit!

On another subject altogether, may I recapitulate on one of the many topics about which you and I have talked, university Christian Unions, which, according to an article in *The Guardian* recently, are the largest societies on many campuses. It added also that "Christians don't seem likely to back-track" which is a reason for thanksgiving!

You will remember we spoke about the place and purpose of CUs and that it is really important when considering any issue, first to locate the historical landmarks and sign-posts. Then we can trace development and track causes for this and that. Probably one of the earliest attempts to bring Christian students together was the founding in the 18th century at Oxford university by John and Charles Wesley of what was derisively known as the Holy Club. During the 19th century, some Christian leaders, such as Charles Simeon at Cambridge, inspired students to take a stand. From small, despised beginnings, specifically evangelical work among students in Britain was floated on 9 March 1877 by the launching of what is now known as the Cambridge Inter-Collegiate Christian Union. Following this flagship, other CU vessels took to the sea of faith. From that flotilla in 1928, IVF (Inter-Varsity Fellowship), now UCCF (Universities and Colleges Christian Fellowship), sailed while in 1947 the keel of IFES (International Fellowship of Evangelical Students) was laid down. The original *principles* on which the CUs were built, remain today. They are student led. They are temporary. They are not churches but they are an arm of the Church with unique evangelistic objectives and opportunities. Each generation of members is confronted by the ever-shifting cultural and social thought of the day, parallelled by current ideas and trends in Christianity. Each year, wise heads need to be screwed on to young shoulders!

It happens from time to time that one may not like everything that takes place in a CU and a choice has to be made: either to criticize from outside or to work for change inside. Most CUs are in good heart. A few show a hesitant hand.

When I visit university or college CUs, I find that all of them contain one or more of the following: a few interested folk who are genuinely looking for reality in Christians' lives; those who became Christians in their early teens who have since slipped back and doubtless are attracted by some of the things most of their fellow students do; those who are religious, tepid and bland, apparently indifferent to passion; those, usually the majority, who are effectual and going full-steam ahead, all guns blazing. I hope yours is among the latter – provided always there is love exhibited alongside the truth proclaimed. Truth and love are two sides of the same coin; they're not to be separated.

The original *purposes* of CUs are the same today as they have always been. They are to present the claims of Jesus Christ to members of the university; to invite and encourage those who intend to serve him; to be committed to God's work world-wide through the Church. To those ends, CUs have found the following *practices* to be sound: excellent regular Bible studies and teaching; joyful fellowship and worship; regular prayer meetings; some thoughtful and credible evangelistic events. Each of these, as you know, has to be considered in the light of current and local circumstances. Today's CUs have different ways of ministering to members and in outreaching. Yet the emphasis on believing and understanding, knowing *and* applying Scripture has to be paramount for growth in godliness and clear, compassionate witness. The New Testament strongly stresses unity in the truth of the gospel but it also condemns partisanship, dividing on secondary matters.

My generation of Christian student friends had a hunger for the word of God, a passion for truth and righteousness. There was prayerfulness and diligence in personal Bible study. We had a strong missionary commitment abroad and at home and a longing for our contemporaries to come to a saving knowledge of Jesus Christ. And for all those who hoped it would be so, it was a surrogate family. Do not think that this means that I view the past as necessarily the best; not at all. The practice of some of those things I've mentioned is not retreat. It is the necessary requirement for advance. For over one hundred years, CU members have proved that. You may be interested to know that many of the CU members who left university the same year as myself have kept in touch for over fifty years through a twice-yearly prayer-news letter and occasional reunions. This has been a rich source of fellowship and an encouragement to keep going. I commend it to your generation as a further means of support and a reminder that we're *all* fighting in the *same* war until our Commander sends for us or until he returns.

I also commend to you a book by the historian Oliver Barclay: *Evangelicalism in Britain 1935–1995*. It is a broad-brush assessment of some of the significant movements during those years and has some valuable things to say about CUs. I'll send you a copy.

One should not lose sight of the fact that the CU has a rôle in the everyday life of the university or college. Recently, the UCCF student magazine *NB*, in its stimulating 'Reality Bites' column, put the following excellent theoretical suggestions to an imaginary Christian Union: encouraging members to get involved in Students' Union welfare activities; supporting regular campaigns in the Students' Union of various justice initiatives which are organised by a secular pressure group; organising their own soup run for local homeless people every Friday night.

By the way, no student can get involved with everything that the CU lays on, if they are to remain sane and get their work done! Thoughtfully and prayerfully try this meeting, try that and then consistently settle on those you think will be helpful to you where also you can be helpful to others. By the same token,be sure to cast your net into the wider cultural and sporting river of the university. Again, be prayerful and sensible. May I suggest that you use as the criterion the many hours you will need to spend on private study of your subject. That should come first, really.

Your predecessors have left you a God-given heritage. Hand on that flag of God's truth to next year's Freshers!

Best wishes

Donald

A BRIEF NOTE

Dear Richard,

I sense you are feeling low now some of the excitement of 'newness' has worn off. Expectation and reality don't always coincide. All the familiar things have vanished. You worry perhaps about putting a foot wrong and feel uncomfortable and sometimes fearful.

I too have known these feelings. But they will pass. From one angle, they remind us to take the Lord fully into our confidence and thankfully appropriate his peace. From another angle, we are deliberately to make a choice: not to let the past put a brake on the present. Make that choice. Get up, get out of that armchair! Go for a brisk walk and make a mental list of your many blessings. Thankfully shout them aloud!

Every good wish and do give me a ring if you want to.

Donald

PS. I am sending you some Chocolate Biscuits!

MENTORING AND SELF-DISCIPLINE

Dear Richard,

Thank you for phoning about the Christian Union and mentioning also that you are no longer thinking of a career in teaching. Of course I respect your decision and you know you can talk about it if you wish. Mentioning this reminds me of an incident that happened on my last day at the school where I'd been teaching on my return from L'Abri Fellowship in Switzerland. I was on my way to see the Headmaster and walking a little ahead of me, unaware of my presence, were two prefects. They were talking and one said to the other, "I'm sorry Drew's leaving", to which the other replied, "Yes, he's a nice bastard!" I was thankful for small mercies!

We talked also about relationships but in the context of your getting to know another student who has recently become a believer. I am glad to hear this and thank you for asking me how you might help him. As you know, I try not to use the word "relationships" on account of its elasticity. Yet I am using it here to mean your getting to know and spending time with your friend young in the faith, he knowing you are trustworthy and a little more experienced, a mentor to whom he may look up. That means meeting regularly which could result in becoming firm friends, while the suggestions that follow may be useful for staying alongside anyone who is interested or seeking. In any event, stay alongside him while you're both at university.

The German pastor Dietrich Bonhoeffer wrote, "The Christian needs another Christian who speaks God's word to him. He needs him *again and again* when he becomes uncertain and discouraged, for by himself he cannot help himself without belying the truth. He needs his brother as a bearer and a proclaimer of the divine word of salvation. He needs his brother solely because of Jesus Christ.. His own heart is uncertain. His brother's is sure". This born-from-experience truth is irrefutable. The young man who led me to repentance and faith in Christ was such a mentor who also introduced me to a number of his Christian friends, a reminder that we're fighting together in the same battle. I find it significant that Jesus chose twelve men to be *with* him.

There are things to share: your homes and families; your mutual or different interests, gifts and studies, playing sport, seeing a film – and thoughtfully evaluating it – having a meal out, these are ways of building trust and affection. As has been said, "So often in our 'Me first' culture, nobody else has bothered to show such interest". When you meet, you meet also to feed little by little on passages from the Bible, intended to build up his – and your! – knowledge and application. Pray through passages and apply them to living. Like the Lord, the Bible is living, powerful and active and your friend will begin to grow into redeemed humanness. Introduce him to some of your friends. Make a note of his address so you can occasionally keep in touch with him during the holidays. As friendship develops, make another note to send him a birthday and Christmas card. Use the telephone as a prayer line! My generation referred to all this as, among other things, Personal Work. Indeed it is for we meet as persons, as persons created in the image of God willing to learn from and build each other up. Having been a Christian longer than he has, you can teach him and at the same time be excited by his learning!

Your friend has become a believer either at a point in time or over a period of time. When any unbeliever becomes a believer, we can say that he or she is a convert, one who has been converted, who has changed direction. But conversion is only the beginning. A convert is a beginner. A disciple is a learner. Assuming his conversion is genuine, he will want to become a disciple, that is, a learner, a follower. You, his mentor and Christian brother, are privileged to lead him "farther up and farther in," to learn and to grow. John Wesley spoke of the Christian as having "the choice of walking in the higher or lower path". You too can aspire to be holy and to go on increasing in the knowledge of God or settle for a less demanding and nominally, still Christian, way of life. Such will also be less rewarding and there is the likelihood that the "voyage of (your lives) will be bound in shallows and in miseries". At the commencement of one's life as a follower of Jesus Christ, a decision must be made: either, as the hymn has it, "All for Jesus" or 'Some for me and some for him.' Present your friend with the consequences of the choices before him.

Like everything in life and certainly in the Christian life, there is a struggle: struggle to distinguish between the important and the urgent, to make time, to meet commitments, to be refreshed and recover one's breath. The first believers, that great multitude spoken of in Hebrews II of men and women through the centuries who have fought the fight, finished the race and kept the faith were ordinary people like ourselves, who strove and fell, but who got up and went on. At the end of his life, did the great apostle Paul smoothly say: "My dear friends, as I look back upon a remarkable life it seems to resemble nothing so much as enjoying cucumber sandwiches on the Vicarage lawn". No he didn't! Each time he fell he got up and went on, got up and went on. To do that, to mean business with God, we must aim at self-discipline with some planning.

That doesn't mean that we should live mechanically but it does mean that we should not leave everything to the last minute, the 'whatever' approach. Paul addresses young Timothy as a soldier of Jesus Christ. And it must be said that the necessary self-discipline and the obedience that is strengthened by its practice do not come quickly. They have to be worked at. If I may carefully say so, your generation knows little about discipline or self-discipline. The same could be said of society generally. Like the Ten Commandments, these attributes are to protect us and our nation, not to restrict us. The Creator who made us knows what is helpful to us and what is harmful. Self-discipline strengthens self-control and lack of either causes a general enfeebling of character. Should self-discipline or any other attribute become only a self-righteous aim, then one's in trouble. That is not what is intended. Self-control and self-discipline are each *positive* attributes that God wants us to covet. They assist in making us more complete people and more effectual followers of Jesus Christ.

You ask how I have set about trying to attain these necessities. I have far from succeeded but I try first to make them the subject of conversation with the Lord; secondly, by not disturbing nor keeping folk waiting because of my unpunctuality; thirdly, by getting up in the morning when my alarm-clock rings. The latter is probably bad news for you or any student but in my opinion is the first and most important step to be taken. Self-discipline is helped also when we occasionally say 'No' to a chocolate-bar! Truly, if you sow these seeds, you and this young follower, other things being equal, will reap a lifetime's reward in profitable Christian service. Other qualities also benefit when we begin to realize that as followers of Jesus Christ we have a responsibility, a charge, a duty to think and behave in a new way. Yet covered with the whole armour of God, and rallied by fellow soldiers, we shall achieve.

In this connection, learn to stand against today's emphasis, which seems especially aimed at young people, on self-esteem. People don't seem to understand that it is impossible to achieve real accomplishments without first possessing self-respect. Feeling good about oneself by no means leads to worthwhile achievements or to self-respect. Self-esteem is a hollow thing. Self-respect, giving everything your best effort in little or big things, will help to increase your self-respect.

But when we fail, as we do, we still get up and go on, get up and go on. Never lose sight of your objective. Learn from certain things but firmly leave each negative past behind. *Never let the past put a brake on the present.* Keep moving in the direction of the goal. It is hard sometimes to do that as I have known and still know– I get tired and I get dulled. Fix your eyes on Jesus who began and finished the journey we're taking together. I've been on it for over fifty years! You may know this verse from a small but stirring Charles Wesley hymn which I sometimes sing after I've finished my Quiet Time: "A charge to keep I have, a God to glorify / A never-dying soul to save to fit it for the sky / To serve the present age, my calling to fulfil / O may it all my powers engage to do my Master's will!" Incidentally, some hymns and songs make excellent prayers.

As the sun is shining, I'm breaking off here to have my daily forty-minute or so brisk walk in the countryside. At these and other times I have found the truth of the writer William Hazlitt's remark that "I am never less alone than when alone". I feel at home in this part of God's creation and in any event the natural world is alive with a variety of sounds and sights while thoughts and memories crowd each other. It is not possible for us to have a *relationship* with nature – except possibly with a horse or a dog – but it is certain that we have an *association*. What do you think? By the way, I hope you have joined the Rowing Club and in this way are not only getting exercise to help you to keep fit but being, although exhausted, deeply satisfied!

All good wishes

Donald

PS. I am sending you also a copy of Steven Garber's book *The Fabric of Faithfulness* which shows the necessity to weave together belief and behaviour during the university years. It's first class.

TODAY'S CONTROLLING IDEAS

Dear Richard,

You'll remember that the last time we had tea together, among other subjects we spoke about the almost magnetic pull between your contemporaries' culture and the desire and need for radical discipleship. Your generation of believers is confronted by ways of thinking and behaving as well as issues that my generation never or hardly ever encountered, because they did not exist. Nowadays, on different occasions and from different people, Christians encounter ostracism, scorn, sarcasm, hostility, indifference, ridicule, mockery, responses you would not meet if you were a Hindu, a Sikh or a Muslim. To some extent, Christians have brought and bring this upon themselves but that's another story.

You began, I recall – having devoured two toasted teacakes! – by saying that you thought that in such situations the first thing to do is consciously, deliberately to remind oneself who one is and whom one serves, sending up an SOS which includes asking for the love of Jesus through you to meet them. You then said one more thing: "In these situations, I make a point of not creating opportunities but seizing opportunities to speak where I feel reasonably comfortable and know what I'm talking about and also that I'm willing to say that I don't know such and such but if they really want to know, I will find out." Both these statements impressed me as showing humility and honesty and being appropriate in a first encounter and as a prelude to further discussions.

May I add to your really thoughtful statements what I think I said at the time? Listen. Pray. Listen. Love. Listen. Find points of contact. Listen. Each of us has some concern for the world and its problems. Whatever we believe, each of us has some interest in knowing if there is any meaning to our lives. Those points of contact are no more than that: just touching. But they're a beginning and should lead to the big questions: who am I? Why am I here? From where did I come and to where am I going? Is there any meaning or purpose in life? What am I for?

Fifty years ago in the western world, the prevailing consensus, the religion and culture were able to be talked about. It is less frequent today and at breath-taking speed has been swamped and superseded by various philosophies and muddled Eastern thought which, taken together, have produced what the writers Charles Colson and Nancy Pearcey, in their book *How now shall we live?* call Naturalism. In simple terms, that means the idea that only nature exists. It means also that there is no God of the Bible who created and sustains the universe (I thought we got as far as this but in case we didn't, I'll go on!). It is within the ideas of Naturalism that most students live and move and have their being. And, ideas have consequences.

As you will know, the idea of Naturalism creates two major consequences. The first is relativism which deduces that as nature is all that exists, then there can be no one final moral truth. There is no moral consensus any more, no agreement on what is meant by 'right' and 'wrong'. This is to be seen particularly in the wide world of the Humanities. So we each make it up for ourselves, and have different and changing opinions on moral issues. As the novelist William Golding said, "If God is dead, if man is the highest, then good and evil are decided by majority vote." The second consequence, multi-culturalism, is that on account of relativism all religions and cultures have equal moral validity. It is said that in the country from which we come and in the gender we have, that we find meaning and purpose in life. Therefore to understand our contemporaries, we must, as Paul did at Athens and in other cities, understand why and how those wrong ideas mould peoples' lives.

This is enough for one letter!

I hope you sense that you are moving in the right direction in your studies – and that your tutor agrees with you!

Every good wish

Donald

PS. A clearly written book on today's culture is Marcus Honeysett's *Meltdown*, which makes sense of our culture in crisis.

GETTING ALONGSIDE STUDENTS

Dear Richard,

Thank you for the telephone call about my last letter.

You said your friend next door "has not mended his ways". I'm not surprised, nor should you be! It's early days. You're committed to the long haul. Each believer is. By the amazing grace of God, we keep going, getting up and going on until God sends for us. Like you, he's a typical student of today, nearing the end of his teens with too much freedom, not much sense yet about money and fearful of not belonging. Stay alongside him and persist in praying for him for the Lord has sent him to you. This does not undercut or modify what I said in my first letters about your not going to university primarily to evangelize your contemporaries! When we last met, there wasn't much time left to talk about 'living' but I recall your stressing that actions, especially unselfish and sacrificial actions, speak louder than words. When you said that, I remembered not only your mate next door but the opportunities you will have in the Rowing Club. There, as elsewhere, your witness is being observed and tested.

Let me try to recapitulate what we said on the phone. By and large, it is only the relational that has any meaning for most of your contemporaries. To win them for Christ, you *get* and *stay* alongside them in your Christian humanness. In my first letter, I spoke about many students' home background who also have not always been helped by their schooling. These and other factors lead them into a foggy uncertainty where they are hurt by pretended humanness, false ideas and painful consequences. For so many folk, there is a huge festering emptiness and sense of futility about life that won't go away. The Lord has sent you (and other followers of Christ) to live among them in the Students' Union bar, in the lab, on the football pitch, to share their pain and show his love.

Getting alongside folk is comparatively easy. *Staying* alongside them is a test, a test of character of which, let me say, you have plenty. This applies not only to your approach to unbelievers but to your friends in the CU and at church. Getting relationships right between men and men, women and women and men and women, and working at them to keep them that way, regularly needs checking. Trying to build relationships doesn't start from scratch. It starts and grows from the soil of loving God with all my passion and prayer, intelligence and energy. This first and always, and not until then will I be able to see other people as lovable and love them. By and large, your contemporaries are indifferent to the ideas of truth and morality. But they do understand and depend on loyal relationships. Many such relationships are untrustworthy, unstructured, unstable, like feathers in the wind, so to find someone alongside them, to have the possibility of a friendship, of real belonging, is manna from heaven. Only love can summon a response of love.

There are other aspects to this matter. You and some other folk see a film and afterwards, as opportunity arises, you speak about its excellencies, its shortcomings, its lies. Saying something when you have the opportunity can be more credible than you might think. God will honour it. Something similar can be effective in the Students' Union over a drink. For some believers, there is an opening for witness in being nominated to the Students' Union committee.

We are not called to be nice to people – we should be that anyway – but carefully challenge them. Amiable religiosity is not only pointless but a hindrance. In the writer Oswald Chambers' words, 'We are not to be poetical but surgical'! Be interested in some of the things your contemporaries are enthusiastic about. Pop culture has its values. There is excellence to be found in some pop culture. Respect its achievements, comment on its failures and falsities. Listen for the meanings, messages and values in pop culture. How are they presented? How would you present the Christian position?

We easily forget that love is the chief outward characteristic of the Christian life. God's love in us should enable your next- door friend and other folk with whom you're friendly to understand that you love him or her for *themselves*, not what they project and certainly not as spiritual butterflies to be caught and pinned! We are not to judge. We are to love, for love is as love does. We are to love unconditionally and that often means making a deliberate and continual choice to love someone, to take that person seriously. We are to get alongside – and stay alongside – these folk and carefully and prayerfully listen to and talk with them with respect and affection. And let you and your friends also reach out to Muslims and other such folk who feel isolated and lonely and struggle to integrate into British life. Some of you have to be there for them.

I really do believe that each separate person you and I meet is needing, above all else, to meet and receive God's love through us, tough yet tender, resilient yet steady, undiscriminating yet involved. Isn't this what Jesus did, identifying with wounded and confused folk, giving much of his time building his life into their lives? Many of your contemporaries are not interested in morality, right or wrong. Yet at the same time they are passionately concerned about matters of justice and equality. There is an opportunity here for discussion and a reminder that it is crucial for believers to have intellectual credibility. This applies also to your having sufficient confidence in the truth of your beliefs, not only because they have intellectual weight and can stand above all other beliefs in the market place of ideas, but just because they are *yours*. In a believer, truth and love are not to be separated. Love is the engine that rides on the rails of truth. The only way to elicit a response to the deep-down hunger for reality experienced by each unbeliever (which is part of God's common grace) is through trust between people. That foundation has first to be laid before a relationship, a friendship can be built.

To a student who asked advice from Augustine, one of the great teachers of the early church, about how to win his friend for Christ, Augustine replied, "Attract him by your way of life if you want him to receive any teaching from you." Admirably does he weigh the scales and point to the consequences: first the living, then the teaching.

The teaching can be summarised under two headings: Jesus the only true Saviour and Christianity the only true world-view. You are getting alongside unbelieving students where they are in their need for real relationships. You are showing Jesus' love, sharing his compassion. That is the beginning. They then must know about Jesus the only true Saviour.

Most people today regard Jesus as just a wonderful man. As the writer Dick Keyes puts it, "One of the reasons Jesus is so widely treated as nice but irrelevant (offering a salvation that nobody really needs) is that people don't really believe the problem exists that he came to solve". The problem is evil. For the average student, fornication, lying, dishonesty – these are not evil, simply part of life. 'I don't need saving. I have problems – we all have. What do I need rescuing from? Jesus is cool, that's all.' So, Keyes continues "evil is miniaturized into disaster or something bad. It's something inexplicable and it's not in people."

This, Richard, is what you have sensitively and determinedly to demolish. At some time, you will be able to bring in John 3: 16 and Revelation 3:20 and cover with prayer. Christianity as the only true world-view perhaps can wait! Yet you need to hold firmly to the fact that the Saviour and the world-view stand or fall together.

Sitting at my desk much of the time can make me sluggish and I need that daily exercise I enjoy – brisk walking. Yet disinclination to exertion seems to have been one of Winston Churchill's traits: "Whenever I feel I should be taking exercise, I lie down until I feel better!" So far, I have been successful in avoiding Churchill's dilemma and hope to continue that way!

All good wishes

Donald

TWO CONFLICTING WORLD-VIEWS

Dear Richard,

I'm delighted that you went to a classical concert and even more that you enjoyed it! From what you said, you not only *heard* the music but *listened* to it and *watched* the players. I'm the same; music has to be listened to, not just heard. Background music? Perish the thought! I'm so pleased and hope you'll go again. Equally interesting was to hear of your talking with a student after a lecture and that she was asking a crucial question: what is the meaning of it all? Then you and the phone ran out of money. Let me put down a few thoughts as a follow-on from our conversation.

The 19th century French artist Gauguin painted a picture famously entitled: *Where do we come from? What are we? Where are we going?* Through the centuries, these have always been the great questions to which different answers have been given. From them, various world-views have been promulgated. One world-view has persisted through the centuries, the Judaeo-Christian. Many other ideas about the world can be summed up in that word Naturalism, the world-view which declares that nature, the seen world and natural causes, are all that there is, while all that can be said about human beings is, to quote the philosopher Jean Paul Sartre, "You are your life and that's all you are." But the Judaeo-Christian world-view declares that there is one world, both seen and unseen, created by a God who has made himself known and can be known. From these two world-views emerge totally different answers to the great questions and usually, totally different ways of living. The one should reveal, in a friend's words, "lives rich in meaning". The other may display "lives of quiet desperation." The former should speak of wholeness and wholesome purpose, the latter may reveal a resignation to survive coupled with a desire for self-gratification.

Before answering Gauguin's three fundamental questions, one must ask a number of prior questions and I'm going to suggest that you gradually work these through and then, if you'd be so kind, give me a ring – and remember to reverse the charge. As British Telecom says, 'It's good to talk!' By the same token, as my brother lives in the west of England, some distance from me, we use the phone a good deal. One day, I'd like you to meet him.

Best wishes

Donald

PRESENTING THE CHRISTIAN POSITION

Dear Richard,

Thank you for phoning. First, let me say how very sorry I am that your father has been made redundant. This is an anxious time for you all. If you think I could help in any way, do let me know. Yet in the midst of your loving concern, have your objectives clearly in sight and keep going for them. Secondly, thank you for agreeing to work through those 'prior' questions I mentioned in my last letter. Indeed it's good to talk when you have something to say, as you had, rather than having to say something! To help you remember what you said, I'll write them down in this letter – assuming you keep some of my letters!

You suggested that the first crucial 'prior question' to ask about a world-view should be: does this world-view fit in with reality as human beings experience it? Spot on. Next you suggested: Is it consistent? Is it testable? Is it reasonable? Is it knowable? Is it liveable? And these too are essential questions to ask.

Naturalism – there's nothing apart from what we see, hear, taste, touch, handle – collapses because it can find no satisfactory answers to these crucial questions. The Judaeo-Christian world-view on the other hand can show that 'Yes' is the answer to all the questions. With some of your Christian friends, why not discuss these?

Following on from that little exercise, keep the ball gently rolling by patiently considering the evidence for the truth and uniqueness of the Judaeo-Christian world-view.

I'm so pleased that you realize the need to help unbelievers to see the emptiness, futility and the falsity of any world-view built on humanistic sand. Alas! there are few students who are willing to consider these matters as the majority appear to have no time for 'truth-claims'. Today's cultural climate does not so much despair of there being no answers as arrogantly assert that there are none. But I have found a useful place to start a discussion are the first four words of Genesis I:I, "In the beginning, God....." announces, I believe, the most significant and magnificent statement in all of Scripture. This should put the cat among the canaries! The existence of God there declared is the necessary presupposition of all truth and of all human dignity and freedom.

Think about it.

Best wishes

Donald

CONFIRMING THE CHRISTIAN POSITION

Dear Richard,

I'm sure you wish I had e-mail! But there it is, I haven't and in any event, I enjoy hearing a voice and having a conversation together. Once more, I am writing down your replies from rough notes I made while we were talking. If you want, you can have them available for future use. Let me add that you and your friends have come up trumps. Well done and thank you Lord! The 18th century theologian, William Paley, was not the first person to produce evidence for the truth and uniqueness of what is called Christianity but you'll be pleased to know that you've made some of the points that he made!

If I may, let me preface your list of 'evidences' with the following statements. Since approximately 1900, if not earlier, the contemporary view of mankind and the universe revolves round the notion of synthesis, that is, the uniformity of natural causes in a closed system. A human being is said to be no different from a cactus or a camel, only matter, a machine for a gene. By contrast, Christianity revolves round antithesis, that is, the uniformity of natural causes in an open system. The infinite, personal God is able to and does intervene in his universe which contains your 'evidences'.

Here's your list taken from my rough notes: the external universe, the natural world, its structure, variety, regularity, unity, continuity, beauty; pure science; biblical archaeology; the existence and history of the Jewish nation; the existence and history of the Christian church; human creativity; unsatisfied longings for something more than the visible and external; the fact of Jesus Christ; the results in lives that are truly changed; the existence of conscience; the effect of true Christianity upon nations and society; the freedom that comes from knowing the forgiveness of sins and a power for proper living; conscience.

All these are evidence for the truth and uniqueness of

Christianity. But evidence alone does not necessarily constitute certainty. It is an indication or a sign, a basis for belief.

None of these 'evidences', sufficient and clear in themselves, is proof. I'm so glad that that is so – God is not a man. See Numbers 23:19; I Samuel 15:29; Ezekiel 28:25; I John 4:12. He does not have to submit himself to human investigation. He is not on trial! Evidence and proof coalesce in him. If I may use the homely proverb, "the proof of the pudding is in the eating." Thank God that we don't have to prove he is there and can rest content with the evidence that has been granted us. Why should we expect to have it all in this life? Let God be God. Proof can wait for eternity.

There is one more thing. I open my Bible and it speaks to me of truths I can find nowhere else. I open my Bible and I find things of which, about the world and myself, I can say, "I know". But more amazing is that my Bible knows *me*! It knows things about me and truths about men and women and the world that no other book can ever know or has ever known.

Yet before enlarging on this subject it's time I said something about postmodernism. But I'll leave it to next time.

All good wishes

Donald

POSTMODERNISM

Dear Richard,

In an earlier letter I wrote about Naturalism which, along with other beliefs and ideas about human beings, has its place on the chess-board of what is called postmodernism. What I am about to say will be compressed but I hope it will do justice to the main issues.

This is not another philosophy or a new religion. Just as on a chessboard there are different players positioned or moving here or there, so postmodernism is characterised by different fashions, beliefs and trends which have, as it were, an independent life yet merge together, then disappear to be replaced by other ideas. The clearest way I can explain this is by quoting the last paragraph of Malcolm Bradbury's novel, *Dr Criminale*, which is in effect, a brilliant definition of postmodernism. The main character is speaking: "Naturally, I would always be tolerant, sceptical, permissive, pragmatic, good-hearted, open ..... I would also assume nothing is true or certain; no ideology, philosophy, sociology, theology any better than any other. Life for me would therefore be a spectacle, a shopping-mall, an endless media show in which everything – amusing or grotesque, erotic or repulsive, heroic or obscene, sentimental or shameful – is an acceptable world-view, and anything could happen. There would be no great wisdom and no great falsehood. A mule would be the equal of a great professor...."

It is not too difficult to see this panoramic jumble of thoughts being acted out in daily life. And, as you have discovered, many, perhaps most, of your contemporaries think and try to live this way. They do so partly in reaction to 200 years or so of belief in the sufficiency of human reason and some of the technology and devastation that it has produced.

But – and this is where believers *must* stand up and be

counted – postmodernism, having denied the sufficiency of human reason, goes on to declare that there is no such thing as revealed truth. The only way to live is by sensations and experiencing whatever takes your fancy. Reason is replaced by experience, feelings and sensations and you express yourself in any way you wish. So once more, truth – which today lies in consensus – has lost out. Without truth, there's no power for change.

Malcolm Bradbury's character is the prototype, the forerunner of today's postmodernists. The novelist William Golding perceived that, "in the second half of the twentieth century one has no surety, no safe solid ground on which to stand; one has to drag out of one's own entrails some kind of validity." That seems even more true now. But the gospel remains unchanged, unchanging, unchangeable and continues to transform peoples' lives. Don't be fazed by the trend, Richard. Hold fast to the truth as it is in Jesus, revealed, as he is, in all the Scriptures.

This emphasis on feelings and expressing oneself may seem exciting until one perceives that the Post–Modernist generation sadly is characterised not only by excessive individualism but by isolation, loneliness and broken relationships, by inconstancy, boredom and anxiety.

In different ways, all of us are affected by the incessant rapidity of change. It has been said that more change has taken place socially, relationally, environmentally and technologically during the last three decades than in the last three centuries. "Like sand castles on the beach after high tide", very little of the past is recognisable and this rapidity minimises it and impairs a reasonable perspective on the future.

As Marcus Honeysett shows, postmodernism has five arrows in its quiver: one, there are no certain ties, no absolutes; two, there is no foundation on which value or moral judgments can be made; three, no human being can ever know if anything is real; four, there is no such thing as human personhood; five, no one can correctly understand the original meaning of any text, be it Shakespeare or the Bible.

Best wishes and give me a ring if you want to meet and talk over some of these issues.

Donald

THE BIBLE'S FRAMEWORK

Dear Richard,

I've recently returned from another speaking visit to Cambridge. Like Oxford, the university is the same size (although the city is smaller) but unlike the busy-ness and stranglehold of traffic from which Oxford suffers, Cambridge still has the feel of a market town set in the Fens. Precious and privileged for me were those three years after the War, especially being a member of Emmanuel College, a Puritan foundation where John Harvard was an undergraduate. Since then, as you know, I've kept in touch with students and on this visit was able to have good talks with some of them. One of these was concerned that he was, among other things, living a Christian life and "doing the right things" but was hazy about the foundations for Christian belief. As I suspected – it is so common – one reason for this was because he was unaware of the significance of the doctrines of the Bible. You have implied that you have the same difficulty. This is going to be a long letter, so put your feet up and take a deep breath!

There are a number of biblical doctrines that permeate and validate the Scriptures. They may be likened to those cast-iron pillars embedded in concrete that support the structures of Victorian piers which jut into the sea at some English seaside resorts. Doctrinal pillars bear the weight of the structures of history, chronology, prophecy, biography and narrative, together disclosing the meaning and purpose of the Bible. The Bible makes certain particular statements – doctrines – that are continued, confirmed and consistent throughout its entirety, for example, the doctrine of God, the doctrine of Assurance. They give us the understanding we need, for which we begin to yearn. Without this foundational understanding, we flounder. With it, we swim.

All these principles stand as a coherent whole; as the theologian, Carl Trueman has said, "to tinker with one part of the scheme requires the modification of the whole." All biblical doctrines hang together. They inform and support each other. Each doctrine is important. No doctrine is more or less important than any other doctrine. They interweave and interlock. Not only is there an indissoluble unity but also a logical inevitability. Another theologian, Stanley Hauerwas says, "If you begin with any doctrine, you will find your way to all the rest." The doctrines may also be likened to a plan, a blue-print for the edifice of Scripture. But although systematic and logical, there is no suggestion of a system, a rigid framework into which the doctrines have to fit.

Through the centuries, the greatest and most influential ministries of people have been and continue to be those whose entire ministry – and not only in the pulpit – was "built on the back of a thorough and thoughtful theological reflection" which leads to biblical preaching and changed lives. The preaching of the Reformers, of George Whitefield, John Wesley, Charles Simeon, C.H. Spurgeon and in our own times, Billy Graham, Martyn Lloyd-Jones, John Stott and Don Carson evidence this. This is a grand reason for getting to grips with this issue.

Another important reason is that because knowledge of doctrine tends to be neglected today, misinterpretations and heresies develop in addition to those that already exist. There have always been folk who either know what God intended to say but didn't or who wanted more than he had said which they supplied! Usually, such people are not deliberately setting out to deceive. Each generation produces its own heresies and one has carefully to pinpoint errors and confirm truth. Each generation – *your* generation, *now* –has to "keep the faith" guarding "the treasure entrusted to *you*" (I Tim. 6:20), for *your* children and *their* children (my italics).

This is essential also for a larger reason. Christianity is *universal* truth and therefore you and I "go on contending for the faith" for the well-being of others. Following Abel's murder by Cain, God asks him where his brother is. Cain's reply is, "Am I my brother's keeper?" The implication of God's response is, "Yes, you are." You and I and all followers of Jesus Christ bear the responsibilities and privileges of having dual citizenship. These great doctrinal pillars are not there to support only you and me. They are essential to support and nourish the nation. In Scripture (I Tim. 3:15), believers are described as the "pillar and foundation of the truth". Never are we to clutch biblical truth to ourselves, retreating into a privatised religion in hope of surviving. We are to be 'up front'. Our nation cannot survive much longer on the straw of self-fulfilment and excessive individualism. Followers of Jesus Christ are, on the one hand, guardians of the truth, on the other hand, guides to the truth. Without these, there are no safeguards for true spirituality and a nation then flounders.

When confessing that 'Jesus is Lord', the first Christians were making a doctrinal statement from which arose a number of questions which required answers. During the early centuries of Christianity, when heresies first appeared, doctrinal statements or creeds were drawn up which were definite and clear. People then as now needed to know what was true and what was false. This is even more necessary than it was in the past because modern media in their various forms rapidly reach millions of people with information about strange ideas, bizarre practices, part-truths and lies, much of which the writer Thomas Carlyle in another context scathingly and rightly denounced as "transcendental moonshine".

Among other things, society's obsession with individual autonomy fosters a great readiness to allow anybody to say anything they like. Whether or not it accords with truth and reality is beside the point. "When I feel good, reality fits into my feelings." I have heard words to that effect again and again. With most of the former signposts obliterated, credibility can be destroyed by credulity, knowledge by ignorance. These things happen daily and especially when media microphones are shoved in front of people's faces who, poor folks, usually do not have something to say but are made to feel they have to say something and so unwittingly and pointlessly pontificate about this or that.

It is frequently assumed that doctrine is like the novelist Walter Scott's prosy antiquarian, Dr Dryasdust. Not so! It may be written drily, it may be taught aridly and if so that is regrettable. Yet doctrine is *thrilling*! It moves me to wonder, followed by awe; I hope it will have a similar effect on you. Biblical doctrines are not exquisite exhibits in a museum. They enshrine enduring truths. These pillars, "the prop and support of the Truth", are not to be contemplated in admiration but applied in practice. You and I daily hear the discordant and despairing notes of today's philosophy, post-modernism. The sound should steady those of us who are believers to keep our nerve and yet remind us of our responsibility to live and speak the truth. Sadly, the notes we hear stress image rather than reality, self-expression rather than self-restraint, feeling rather than reason.

Emphasis on the visual rather than the verbal, plus the results of deconstruction also present challenges to defenders of the faith. In addition, vindication of the truth has to be made in view of ecumenicalism, New Age ideas and the mushrooming cults. Moreover, as the historian Oliver Barclay has observed, "When doubt is cast on doctrinal certainties, it will not be long before the same uncertainty applies to ethics" and this is happening. Some of the great creeds and confessions were purchased for you and me through appalling suffering and even eventual martyrdom. The theologian J. I. Packer has written that "the Christian life is cross-country travel all the way with hedges and ditches, ups and downs, rough places and smooth places, deserts and swamps. There are storms and fogs punctuating the sunshine. *The purpose of the map* is to enable the walker to find the true path. With a good map, he will recognise the terrain around him, *relate the features he observes to the larger landscape* (my italics) and see at each stage which way he should go." The Bible's doctrines are intended to and achieve that end.

I would like to send you the preacher Martyn Lloyd-Jones' three paperback volumes in his *Great Doctrines Series*. They are a gold-mine. The writer A.M. Hodgkin's *Christ in all the Scriptures* I will also send. One's student years are a good time to build up a Christian library that will be of use to you throughout your life.

May I suggest another helpful thing: if a book has no index, on the end papers make your own for future reference – subjects, topics, book titles, places, people, etc. You'll find it invaluable.

This is a formidable letter in the sense that I have written at length about an important and gloriously rich subject. The word 'formidable' calls to mind a couple of whom I heard who were on safari somewhere in Africa. They were in the bush and the wife, a strong-minded, well-upholstered lady, whom the French would call *une femme formidable*, wandered off on her own and appeared to be cornered by a wildebeest. Distraught friends asked the husband what he proposed to do. "Nothing," he snapped. "He got himself into this position. He can get himself out of it!"

Best wishes

Donald

YOUR MOST PRECIOUS POSSESSION

Dear Richard,

I trust that your work is moving on well even though I dare say you feel bowled over by the amount that faces you. Then you may agree with this observation: "The more I study, the more I know. The more I know, the more I forget. The more I forget, the less I know. So why study?" Be that as it may! when studying do remember to oxygenate your brain every half-hour or so by sticking your head out of the window, otherwise drowsiness will make you sluggish.

I trust that the CU is in a healthy state. I regularly pray for you all. You are good to bear with me as I jump from topic to topic! This is not done on impulse but what I consider at the time to be important as well as certain things about which you say you are thinking. By the way, I'm looking forward but only if it's convenient for you, to hearing from you about meeting again some time.

It is a fact today that among too many Christian students (as amongst most unbelieving students), there is an alarming ignorance of biblical truth partly caused by unhelpful and even cavalier attitudes towards the Bible. Many students also appear to have gained little knowledge of the Bible at school or even from church. Most of them come from non-Christian homes. When I consider the firm grounding in the Scriptures that my contemporaries and I received in the Christian Union and the often sacrificial way which enabled them to be given, I am saddened as well as alarmed, not only at the widespread superficial knowledge but also an apparent indifference to the supremacy of the Scriptures in student and other circles. We came to love and to learn from the Bible, in particular its doctrines. It shaped then and does now, our ideas of Christian service. It was a rock for our ethics. It powered our preaching. It was the handbook for personal work, one-to-one. It piloted us through hard times.

Spiritual giants, if I may call them that, like Norman Anderson, Basil Atkinson, Donald Grey Barnhouse, Duncan Blair, Godfrey Buxton, Stuart Holden, Martyn Lloyd-Jones, Donald MacKay, G. Campbell Morgan, Graham Scroggie, Rendle Short, William Still, L.F.E. Wilkinson among others, faithfully and lovingly taught it. They are probably only names to you, but they and many like them who fought the fight, finished the race and kept the faith, are an honoured part of Christian history and enabled us to see that the Bible is not a religious text swarming with pious platitudes. It is a God-given practical handbook for everyday living for every person and declares itself to be the only truthful world-view.

As from time to time I am privileged to go to speak at CUs, I find that there seems to be plenty of faith, or what appears to be faith, but even that sometimes seems to be assembled on a paucity of knowledge. Equally important to knowing and comprehending the Bible for growth in personal living is to develop a biblical world-view, to view all aspects of knowledge and areas of life in the light of eternity. *That automatically includes the subject you are studying.* After God has touched my spirit, the Bible's message throughout is primarily addressed to my mind, to my understanding. Despite what some writers – D.H. Lawrence is an example – and contemporary thinking may assert, the emotions cannot apprehend Truth. *Clichés* about 'being true to my feelings' – I say this gently – are nonsensical. Truth has *first* to be apprehended by the mind. Emotions may then confirm it. It is not intended that I shall have only a succession of warm or ecstatic experiences, although from time to time I shall be affected by emotion and experiences and be moved by the Holy Spirit to praise and thank God for who he is and who he is to me.

The temperature reading for assessing the state of my spiritual life is *not* that of subjective experiences and feelings. If it were, the reading would alternate between rocketing or plummeting! Folk in the cults and contemporary 'spiritual' movements are too eagerly experiencing experiences. The correct reading is my growing knowledge of and increasing love for God through Christ, wanting moment-by-moment to live for him. Allied to this, there is a danger for evangelism to become need-centred to the point where repentance and submission to Christ are pushed to one side. Our culture is experience-directed and need-centred. Our preaching, to be biblical and faithful to its listeners, must be thoroughly Bible-based and Christ-centred.

I hope you are finding a growing desire to open up the Scriptures and, as it were, just fall into them! Open the Bible like any other book. But remember it is unique. It is not *a* book. It is *the* book (which is what the word 'Bible' means), made up of sixty-six books. Neither is it a haphazard collection of ancient wise sayings nor good advice. It is not the most remarkable of the world's sacred books. It is not a message in a bottle washed up on a beach. Nor is it a book that *contains* the Word of God. The Bible *is* the Word of God. This letter is not the place to substantiate the last two statements. Sometime we may talk about it.

Then what is the Bible, you ask? It is one book. It is one book with one theme about one person. That person, Christ, is either explicitly or implicitly spoken of in each book of the Bible. God guiding the writers is its author, translators sometimes its martyred messengers. Receive it thankfully. Do not read it lightly. *Feed* on it! As you progress, you will find that you are somehow maturing, peace and joy are slowly accruing, usefulness in his service is gradually increasing. There will be occasional times of dryness, yet the wonder and preciousness of what God has given us in this book should keep on increasing. The theologian Francis Schaeffer knew this. If he woke during the night, so precious was his Bible to him that sometimes he would reach out to touch it. Martyn Lloyd-Jones, preaching about the Bible, said, "I do not put forward theories and philosophies. I start on this premise: that what I am announcing is what I find in the Bible... I am utterly dependent on it." That is the voice of sanctified common-sense and spiritual discernment.

Today, I have reason to wonder how many Christians *daily,*

regularly feed on the Scriptures or even read them. Meditate, reflect on things in your mind. To meditate is not simply to understand the meaning of the words. It means taking time to think over, consider from different angles, digest, puzzle out and visualise, to revolve the words in one's mind. I think this is a neglected discipline and fear that something similar is true of prayer, especially persistent prayer. The speed of life in an image culture conspires against these necessities. They are out of fashion, as though that mattered. What does matter is that my life and yours as followers of Jesus Christ are dependent on the efficacy and practice of these things. Just as each morning a banker turns to the financial pages of his newspaper, a race-horse owner to the sporting pages, so a believer turns to the Scriptures.

The contents of this book are totally different from all the statements concerning the world's religions and cults, philosophies and psychologies. The Bible's teaching is not a philosophy one takes up. It is not a rag-bag of unrelated ideas one holds. It does not provide a DIY approach on how to save your own soul or anybody else's. It is an atlas of salvation, a chart of redemption. There are steps and stages which lead on with logical inevitability. A Christian is one who has been gripped by, and continues to grip, the truth. And that is *always* something rational which also moves one to the depths. It is suffused with feeling because it is about the Great Rescue Operation from sin, Satan and self. The follower of Jesus Christ is freed from the levers and power of manipulation that the world in its various ways exercises. Going with the flow is no longer an option. As the theologian John Stott has phrased it, "the supernatural event of the New Birth has extricated us from the world's control and placed us within the family of God." Have you read C.S. Lewis' Narnia stories? The White Witch's spell has been snapped!

The Bible tells us that we need to be rescued – 'saved' – to come to know God and to demonstrate that he is there. We are not saved to make ourselves into mighty soul-winners. We are not saved to become great preachers. We are not saved to become powerful writers. But we are saved from the guilt, power and pollution of sin to know and love God, demonstrate that he is there and so bring glory to his name in order that our contemporaries may be "brought out of darkness into light." And he saves not a part of you or me but every part of us. The Gospel is for the *whole* man, the *whole* woman, body, mind and spirit. With good news like this, no wonder the reformer Martin Luther declared that, "If you knew what you've been saved *from*, you would die of fear. If you knew what you have been saved *for*, you would die of joy."

The paramount purpose of a CU is to present the claims of Jesus Christ to members of the university. A practical test of whether you and your fellow members know your way about the Bible is if a student wanted to become a Christian now, would you know which Bible verses to show him or her? Conversion is a serious once-in-a-lifetime experience. Do you know the Scriptures that speak of conversion's three parts: conviction of sin, of repentance which leads to faith and then gradually to godliness or holiness of life? Less nowadays is the need for conversion preached as it was when I was a student. More are various *needs* addressed. Or, it is said, Jesus waves us on to higher aspects of human consciousness; or we get lost in the maze of various 'spiritualities'; or one needs to take one's religious convictions, confirmation or church membership more seriously. Not only are such easy-believisms false to the Gospel. They also short-change the believer by giving a false sense of security. I'm sure you won't hear these kind of things at the church you've found. None of these approaches, not even those emphasising 'commitment' to Christ or 'coming to Christ' has anything necessarily in common with the gospel of salvation from sin through the death of the living Christ. The hymn writer Horatius Bonar understood that when he wrote, "'Twas *I* that shed the sacred blood / *I* nailed him to the tree / *I* crucified the Christ of God / *I* joined the mockery." *That* is the truth. *This* is what a man or woman needs initially to hear.

I have made this letter, as the French writer Blaise Pascal said, longer than usual because I lack the time to make it shorter —also because it's supper time!

Every good wish,

Donald

PS. Thank you for letting me know that Lloyd-Jones' and Hodgkin's books have arrived. Now's the time to begin building up that library!

ALWAYS YOUR MOST PRECIOUS POSSESSION

Dear Richard,

Let me push out from shallow water and sail on to the deep with some questions! Just as from time to time our physical bodies need a medical check-up, so do our spiritual parts. When you feed on the Scriptures, do you sense their supernatural power? Do you believe that you owe to the Bible the same reverence – which is not the same as worship – that you owe to God? Do you believe that the triune God is speaking directly to *you*? Let me ask you: do you appreciate that Jesus' attitude to the Bible has to be *your* attitude to the Bible? Are you convinced that the written word (the Bible) and the living word (Jesus) stand or fall together? If you have a wobbly view of Scripture, you will have a weak view of Christ. Should you have an unclear attitude to Jesus, you will have an uncertain attitude to Scripture. To put it bluntly: if you have doubts about Christ or the truth of the Bible, then their authority over you will be negligible. I am sure that you realize what that means: that there will be no authority at all. As you can see, these are really important matters and at full speed, I've hit you with them! But take your time, a long time if necessary, to think and pray through some of these questions, on your own or with some friends.

Sometimes God asks us to believe things that seem to be above reason. But thinking them through, we find they are not contrary to reason. Yet the more we penetrate the truths in the Scriptures, the more we realize that there are some things we do not understand. There are some things we shall never understand. And, as Martyn Lloyd-Jones said, there are also some things that we are *not meant* to understand. God tells us that "things which are revealed belong to us and to our children always". But there are "secret things", ultimate explanations, which "belong only to the Lord our God." Thus we are not foolishly, arrogantly to reject what we do not understand. There is no such thing as an infinitude of the human mind. That should not disturb us at all but rather move us to realize that God, not our limited comprehension, is sovereign. To understand implies standing under. We should stand under, not sit on, the authority and teaching of Scripture. And when we stand under, then we begin to understand. We submit to it as learners.

We also respect God's silences as well as his sayings. We can trust him. The Bible does not say all we would like it to say. But it does say all that God wants to say and all that we need to know. As Francis Schaeffer expressed it, "The Scriptures do not provide exhaustive knowledge. But they do provide sufficient knowledge". We cannot grasp the infinite through finite reason. But when we are willing to submit our minds to God, we shall find that gradually we do comprehend what we need to comprehend. The 18th-century French mathematician and theologian Blaise Pascal correctly said that "the last stage of reason is to realise that there are a myriad things which it does not encompass and it is weak if it does not recognise this. If this is true of the natural world, what can one say of the supernatural?" Moreover, although there is never anything mystical (in the Eastern sense of the word) about the Bible, there is mystery. It seems that mystery is an embarrassment to the modern mind. Some people foolishly equate it with absurdity. Again, that is not so. Why should it be? The great fact is that God is sovereign. Our response should be that we humbly accept the fact that, as the apostle Paul says, that now we see imperfectly but the time will come when we shall understand fully. Remember that there is no God but God. Let us be content to let God be God.

Ask the Lord to help you to honour and apply the Scriptures. A line from the Coronation service states that the Bible is, "the most valuable thing that this world affords." The late Lord Denning (Chief Judge of Civil Justice) remarked that his Bible was "the most tattered book in my library." Scripture gives us steady understanding, not effervescent experiences. It starts to unite our fractured human-ness and begins to shape godliness. No wonder the creed of earlier generations was "The word and the Spirit". They maintained an evenness between the effect of the one and the work of the other in the believer's life.

Luther wrote that "when the believer clings to God's word and promises and makes judgments on the basis of that word, then help and comfort will surely follow." They follow because God realizes that from time to time each of us requires a different impetus or flavour to supply our differing human and spiritual needs. He has provided for that. As required, we encounter the Bible as light and a lamp, rain and snow, fire and heat, a hammer, honey, seed, meat, a sword, milk. Will not these provisions produce health and growth? They will, as I have found over the years despite deliberate wrong-doing, foolishness and faithlessness. The Lord has never let me go and never will. We are debtors to his grace only, Richard.

In conclusion, I ask you to ask some further questions as I do of myself. Don't be alarmed by the questions! They are not intended to plunge you into despair but to lift the eyes of your mind to the God who enlightens. Why not ask them among a group of your friends? Have a few study sessions. But again, take your time; quietly, steadily work through them.

Here they are: What is your attitude to the Bible? Does it need changing? Have there been necessary changes in your life that are forging a closer walk with Christ? Are you asking God to help you widen your biblical horizons as well as enlarge your Christian vision? Are you placing yourself unreservedly in Jesus' hands for him to do with you whatever he knows is best for you? Are you dealing biblically and honestly with any sinful, doubtful or compromising matters there may be in your life? Are you wiser in the ways of God than you were this time last year? In all these things, it is "the entrance of (God's) words that give light" for "only in (his) light do we see light." Yet allow me to give a solemn warning: unless you and I and all believers regard our open Bible as *our most treasured possession* to be loved, believed and obeyed, we are *unlikely to make any significant progress* as followers of Jesus Christ. Along with the great VIctorian preacher C.H. Spurgeon, I can truly say that "I love my Bible.... because it has the blood of Tyndale on it....." I cannot sufficiently stress the importance and necessity of day by day feeding on the Scriptures. Without this daily discipline, one will spiritually wither and die, adapt to contemporary thinking and living and go with the flow, when one could have continued to see God make a positive difference in one's contemporaries' lives.

The Bible translator William Tyndale and others gave their lives so that, in addition to "triggering literacy", ordinary people could find there the truth for themselves. Up to the end of the Second World War, human reasoning had diluted faith in the truth of the Scriptures, while in recent years human reason has for many been abandoned and "what feels right" has taken its place.

These questions I mentioned earlier have brought to mind an incident that occurred when I was sitting one of my History finals. The exam had started. I had already begun to write when the silence was cracked as a late student strode in, swishing his way to the vacant desk alongside mine. Glancing at him, I saw he was a big chap dressed in tweeds and wearing a bow-tie whose appearance suggested he might be more at home on a race course than a History course. Sitting down and seizing the question paper, he perused first one side, then the other, crushed it into a crumpled ball, threw it on the desk, grabbed his gown and strode swiftly out of the hall. Perhaps he had other things on his mind!

That having been said, how are *your* studies going?

Best wishes

Donald

PS. I'm sure you do whatever you can to encourage your Christian friends day by day to feed on the Bible. Such concern by itself can really help them.

A POSTSCRIPT

Dear Richard,

This is a PS to my last letter which contained a fair number of questions. Do I hear your saying: 'Where can I find the time?' Briefly, part of the answer to that question is ruthlessly to examine what creates the busy-ness of your daily life. Are you in overall control? 'In some things, no. In others, yes, and I can eliminate this or that.' It is, I know, a running battle between the urgent and the important. One has to keep on trying to separate them.

Practising what he preached made John Wesley God's man to his generation, an example to subsequent generations. His self-discipline and thoroughness got him up each day at 4.30 am for his Quiet Time and this continued while a student at Oxford and throughout his life. He seems not to have wasted a moment unnecessarily. Wesley would have been a hard but kind mentor!

I hope this extract from one of his sermons will cheer and challenge you as you apply what you can:

"In his presence, I open, I read his Book ... I lift up my heart to the Father of Light: Lord, is it not thy word? "If any man lack wisdom let him ask of God"... thou hast said, "If any man be willing to do thy will, he shall know." I am willing, let me know thy will. I then search after and consider parallel passages of Scripture, 'comparing spiritual things with spiritual'. I meditate thereon with all the attention and earnestness of which my mind is capable. What I learn, that I teach."

Winter is striding into our lives, chilling our bones! But for those of us who are blessed with and thankful for good health, is it not bracing and invigorating?

Every good wish.

Donald

A UNIQUE PRIVILEGE

Dear Richard,

Now I've finished listening to the Fourth Symphony of a British composer, George Lloyd, whose modern music yet resonates with harmonies and melodies, I can concentrate on enjoying writing to you but not before posing a well-known conundrum I've not yet been able satisfactorily to answer: when do we hear music? Until the last note has sounded, it is incomplete. As soon as it sounds, it is already over!

As you know, I pray for you and many others each day and as I was thinking about what to write, your letter arrived asking for my thoughts about prayer.

Prayer is indispensable. Why that is so, we may ask but that it is so, the Bible assures us. It is an indispensable gift from God and the Scriptures give many examples of its use and tell us we too must use it. I find it fascinating that the word 'prayer' contains the idea of being face-to-face with someone. So unless there is a sudden need or emergency, we do not rush into God's presence with our anxieties and needs. Prayer is talking to our heavenly Father, having a quiet conversation with him. We think that we have initiated this but God in his graciousness has done so. We can talk with him in any place at any time about anyone or anything. One of the boys I once taught, whom I had the privilege of leading to Christ, entered the Royal Navy. Part of his duties as an officer was to do the daily rounds of the ship. One of the sailors in the engine room was a believer and unheard in the roar of the engines, these two young men prayed. Each was briefly encouraged by the fellowship and knowing to whom they were speaking and that their prayers would be answered. They could not do without it. None of us can.

The Scriptures are stuffed with passages about prayer, tokens of God's faithfulness and mercy for us whether we pray singly or together. Incidentally, in my opinion, when Christians meet together it should be the most natural thing in the world to pray together. As the poet George Herbert knew: "And though my hard heart scarce to thee can groan / Remember that thou once didst write in stone." Do we pray because, as the poet Alfred Tennyson wrote, "Prayer changes things"? I hope not because it does not. Prayer is not psychology. Neither is it magic. It changes nobody. It changes nothing. It is *God* who, in response to his gift of prayer, changes people and changes things. He not only hears; he listens. He not only listens; he answers. And because only he can see the end from the beginning of our lives – and all the in-between – only he knows when and how to answer. But *always* will he answer.

George Müller's name is a by-word, certainly throughout the English speaking world, for faith in God's faithfulness in answering prayer and in everything else. In the 1830s, this German immigrant to Britain longed to have visible evidence that "our God and Father is the same faithful God as ever he was". For sixty years – and the work continues still on the same principles – he prayed for every penny of the costs for building five large orphanages in Bristol which housed, fed and clothed thousands of children. In our own time, Francis and Edith Schaeffer founded L'Abri Fellowship on similar principles. God *never* lets us down nor lets us go nor plays games with us because he *cannot* do any of these things. Occasionally it may seem – but it never is – that God is absent or arbitrary. He *never* is. We have nothing to fear for present or future – except when we forget that God has led us in the past.

Let me suggest that you read the Scriptures aloud. Its message enters through ears as well as eyes. You can put your emphasis on certain words. You can pause, perhaps in mid-sentence, to think through what you've read.

Following thoughtful 'feeding on' the Scriptures and perhaps asking questions like: what has been said about God? What seems to be the main thrust? What have I learned? Turn each of your answers into prayer.

Here is a suggested pattern of prayer that I find useful and you may also.

Remind yourself into whose intimate presence you are being called. Be quiet. Be still and know that he is God. Think of some of the attributes of God's character stated in the Scriptures. Praise, commend, admire the excellence, the merits, the worth of God. Then confess – not admit, which is having it dragged out of one – your sin, your wrong-doing and wrong-being, those sins that are a burden to you. Plead for forgiveness, for a closer walk with God, for holiness, godly thinking and living. Thank him for his unceasing forgiveness and faithfulness, unfailing loving-kindness and mercy. Then intercede, plead for people, organisations, concerns which feature on your prayer list. From time to time, I conclude by singing or saying a verse or two from one of the old hymns that are packed with biblical truths. During the day, I keep in touch by frequent talking, aloud if possible, to the Lord about this and that. During all the years I have been a believer, I can truthfully say that I have never tired of this routine. I myself have often been stale but never this approach. But find what suits *you*.

I wince when I hear students addressing God as though he were a mate, or 'the guy in the sky' or 'JC'. I do not think that this casualness is intended to be disrespectful. But God – unless there is that urgent need at once to cry out – should be approached in a hugely reverential, respectful way. By the same token, let us think twice before we start 'claiming' this or that from God. I once heard a preacher pray, "We demand...." I appreciate his earnestness. But we have no claims whatsoever on God and are in no position to make any demands. We cannot do better than imitate generations of our forbears who approached the throne of grace with humility and a deep sense of awe yet with confidence, pleading and entreating God for this or that.

Unless in us there is some consciousness akin to fear that God is a holy God and a God of judgment, I doubt whether we have any true perception of who God is and who we are before him. Yes, he is our Father before whom we come to praise and ask in humility and confidence. But he is also unique: the one, only, true, living, eternal, infinite, sovereign creator God, Father, Son and Holy Spirit. Therefore Isaiah's terror (Is. 6:1–5) on account of sin before a holy God should be set alongside Paul's confidence. Scripture clearly speaks of "the exceeding sinfulness of sin". Let us remember that one day we shall bow before him, first as judge. Luther gently rebuked the scholar Erasmus by saying, "Erasmus, your thoughts of God are too human". When writing about the person of God, the writer Thomas Carlyle was right to speak of "the immensities and profundities". God is both father and judge.

We live in the same world as those outside Christ. When you and I read a newspaper, listen to the radio or watch TV and if the news is of personal affliction or group crisis, conflict or confrontation, should we not instinctively cry to the Lord for those concerned? When hearing the sound of fire-engines or ambulances, should we not pray for those in distress? When we are daily confronted by evidence of the world's characteristics which the writer Henri Nouwen pin-points as "self-seeking, manipulation, lying, subterfuge, lasciviousness, cruelty, injustice, power-craving", should we not pray for those suffering from such sinfulness and also for those perpetrating such evil? God's way of fighting evil and restoring truth, order and beauty in individuals, communities and nations, is to make Christians. He has no other agenda, no other way! In a world that has fallen from its original state, the most that people and nations can do is to paper over the cracks. That must ever be attempted or achieved. Then there can be some progress. But there will never be perfection. When we see the results of evil in its various forms in bruised and beaten-down lives, should we not cry to the Lord for those people and for our nation and those known to us? I wonder: do the generality of believers have the deep concern and something of the unswerving passion of John Knox whose prayer was: "Give me Scotland, or I die". What breadth of vision! What depth of request! We are assured that "the prayers of all the people of God (are placed) upon the altar....."

Everything I have said in this letter is addressed to you, Richard. But nearly everything I have said may be applied to a CU or any group praying, worldwide. I recall your telling me recently of the Lesbian and Gay Society disrupting a CU meeting and that most of you continued praying while a few persuaded the LGS to leave. Perhaps some of you had had wind of what was anticipated and wisely and in a godly way dealt with the situation. It might have turned nasty but it didn't for which grateful thanks to the Lord again. I remember saying to you that the CU might consider some follow-up, if possible one-to-one. Public meetings or debates bring issues to the fore but in my opinion are seldom efficacious in the long run. If properly and prayerfully handled, 'friendship evangelism' may result. I hope it does, for it's often the better way.

This letter is approaching the sermonic and as I don't want that and I'm sure you don't, I'll stop! Last week, I went to the Monet Exhibition in London and delighted again in his gorgeous use of light, mist and reflections. I still think he overdid the haystacks and as for the water-lilies, I never want to see another one! But for a brief time, he kept the incessant noise and ceaseless ebb and flow of human life at bay. E.M. Forster, in his novel *Howards End*, has a character remark that "London only stimulates; it cannot sustain". This is what I find, yet I know of others who find that it does also sustain.

All good wishes

Donald

ALWAYS A UNIQUE PRIVILEGE

Dear Richard,

Seated at my desk and looking through the window, I'm looking longingly at a little black Labrador puppy being taken for a walk, or rather taking her owner for a walk. Stretching and straining, twisting and turning, she reminds me of a happy succession of dogs with which for many years I grew up. I'd love to have one again but it would be too much of a responsibility.

I hope you weren't overwhelmed by the contents of my last letter! May I suggest you take it –and this one – in small doses to think over and pray over and really absorb because "prayer is the Christian's vital breath, the Christian's native air." As I said, it's indispensable.

In the midst of your busy student life, try to make time to be quiet, to be still. This will be hard, very hard! But it is a beneficial discipline for the future. It seems to me that noise is one of today's most infectious plagues. It penetrates everywhere and smothers us. In the demented whirl of daily life, we need the regular absence of presence, of stir. Intrusive noise from many quarters hems us in, indeed, at times, assaults us. We should try hard to keep as much of it as we can at arm's length. As Mother Theresa said, "…. (God) cannot be found in noise and restlessness. God is the friend of silence." In this context, why not consider occasional fasting? Let silence and solitude be the circumference, prayer and fasting the centre. Provide a time as Jesus said, "to come away by yourself to a quiet place and rest a while." Luxuriate in the bounty of silence. For that, you need solitude. We all become frayed and fractured because of the frenetic rush of daily life and to forestall that falling-apart, silence and solitude are essential, not optional, essential. The mind and spirit conjoined can then recollect, repent, resolve. Our whole being can become more concentrated on "the things that cannot be shaken," "the things which are not seen", as we "humble ourselves under the mighty hand of God" and again find him unfailingly to be "the lifter up of (our) head".

There have been occasions in my life when I don't feel like praying, don't want to pray, even don't intend to pray. Such petty rebelliousness is, I know, not only wrong but evidence of Satan's power and desire to thwart Christ's work in me, an attempt to cut off communication with God. Every time, I've felt ashamed until I've repented and talked to the Lord about it and recalled that Jesus is "interceding for (me)" particularly "in those agonising longings that cannot even find words." There are times too when I don't feel as though I have been worshipping, praying or pleading but rather presenting requests and reciting lists of names with sincerity but perhaps not really in truth. At these times, it makes all of a good difference to surround the situations and names with appropriate Bible verses. Among the helpful things that a young man in the office where I worked many years ago told me, was the preacher Samuel Chadwick's warning concerning the enemy: "The one concern of the devil is to keep Christian believers from praying. He fears nothing from prayerless work, prayerless religion. He laughs at our toil, mocks at our wisdom. But – he trembles when we pray". To keep believers from praying is certainly one of Satan's priorities as the writer C.S. Lewis reminds us in *The Screwtape Letters.*

Prayer sometimes is hard work. We feel inert, we sound dry, we 'go through the motions'. In other words, we are subjectively absorbed instead of objectively directed. Deliberately let us rouse ourselves, even raise our voices and plead for his grace. The poet John Donne is an encouragement here: "His mercies are ever at their maturity; we ask (for) our daily bread and God never says, 'You should have come yesterday'. He never says, 'You must come again tomorrow.' But *today* if you will hear his voice, *today* he will hear you... All occasions invite his mercies and all times are his seasons."

Other difficulties may occasionally arise such as what appears to be unanswered prayer. Gently, I would say that there is no need to be anxious. It does appear that way. But recall the nature of the character of God: when I'm sure about the truth of the glorious attributes of God's character, I can be sure about *everything* else. In this matter, I can be sure that God loves and listens and answers. As he will not be trifled with so he will not trifle with you. You have his word. You may be hard-pressed, even desperate. But you have his word. God *cannot* lie and therefore does not lie.

Following World War II, relations between the former USSR and the West were like cat and mouse. The USSR was intent on pushing the boundaries of the Soviet empire as far west as possible and blockaded, thus isolating, Berlin. The Allies did not want an armed confrontation but several million human beings were without food, heating and other necessities. In July 1948 the Berlin Airlift began, the Allies initially dropping 3,000 tons a day of food, coal, clothing and sweets for the children. By the end of the Airlift 317 days later, 8,000 tons a day was being dropped. God promises not only relief but provides rescue too.

Prayer is a gift from God to each believer. It is not a device designed by him to discover what we need. That he knows already. He wants us to pray because that strongly expresses our trust in, love for and dependence on him. He is entitled to all that. We pray in faith and humility knowing that he not only delights in listening to us but intends to answer us in his own way, in his own time, for his own best purposes for us, for his everlasting glory. An essential purpose of prayer is to draw us nearer to God for Christ-likeness and for him to do with us what he will.

The evangelist John Wesley's prayer addresses this: "I am no longer my own but yours. Put me to what you will. Put me to doing, put me to suffering. Let me be employed for you or laid aside for you, exalted for you or brought low for you. Let me be full, let me be empty. Let me have all things, let me have nothing. I freely and wholeheartedly yield all things to your pleasure and disposal...." What a prayer! Let us not use it until we mean it. And then let us use it often with growing trust and love for God.

Prayer, as I've said, is one of God's ways to draw us nearer to him. But I have no doubt whatsoever that the *principal* purpose of prayer is to bring glory to God's name. When we discover this is happening, that we are really to be "to the praise of his glory", then our contemporaries and fellow citizens should want what they see we have and are. Your Christ-likeness, my Christ-likeness, poor as it is, is then seen to be for those without Christ's likeness.

Each time you pray, pray in the name of Jesus. This will help to prevent prayer deteriorating into a duty. It will stop discouragement from swamping you. It will focus your mind and heart. Pray as Scripture also enjoins, believingly. Pray with true humility blended with quiet confidence. Pray persistently, not because God is deaf but because he wants to reach deeper into our lives. Pray when you feel like it, pray when you don't feel like it. Pray thankfully because *God is listening*. Pray persistently. Do not build a Folly, a building abandoned when partly completed. Pray perseveringly. Thank God that we can pray about ourselves, about anyone, anything, anytime, anywhere. Persistent prayer prevails!

Moreover, prayer allied to feeding on the Scriptures creates spiritual growth and character refinement which are slow processes but certain ones, for these cause the roots of life in Christ to go deep and to bear fruit in our lives. Without this silent process of deep, gradual growth, we shall remain Christian pygmies instead of attaining to "the stature of the fullness of Christ." But with it, God will use us to his glory in the lives of others. Yet, as the writer Oswald Chambers has said, "the only way we can be of use to God is to let him take us through the crooks and crannies of our own characters". From time to time open yourself up to him, Richard. Let God deal with the mental, psychological, sexual and immoral toxins that harm us. This work of his brings fresh spiritual health and growth. Looked at from another angle, that of Aristotle,who wrote, "the unexamined life is not worth living".

What happens to us when we do not pray? We dry up, we shrivel, we are more easily tempted and more prone to sin. Self-centredness takes over. These are my experiences, as they are for most believers, until we come to our senses and again humble ourselves before God. Without it, as James Fraser, a former missionary in China, says in another context, we are "like a man who has his boat grounded in shallow water. Pull or push as he may, he will not be able to make his boat move more than a few inches. But let the tide come in and lift his boat off the bottom – then he will be able to move it as far as he pleases, quite easily and without friction."

It will not surprise you to know that many books on this subject have been written. What I have offered you are a few crumbs from the bountiful table of prayer. Of the many past or present books on prayer, move heaven – or at least earth – to get hold of O. Hallesby's *Prayer*. I think it's magnificent!

Every good wish

Donald

PS. In the fourth paragraph, I have used the word 'repented' and have a suspicion that, like a number of other biblical words, its meaning today is unclear. It means more than being sorry but it includes that. Repentance means to think again, to change one's mind, to have an abhorrence of sin and heartily to amend one's ways.

KEEPING THE LINES OPEN

Dear Richard,

I think my cold has finally gone. I *hate* colds! They make me grumpy and a silly sort of petty resentfulness possesses me. Again, I realize that, as Shakespeare said, "I am not ague-proof." I hope you are well and keeping fit and persevering in trying to balance the different obligations, desires and responsibilities that push and shove each other about and outside and inside us.

Thank you for taking the time to ring. Talking about Prayer over the telephone and using the phone for praying with someone should by no means be unusual. I am glad though that my last letter gave you a good deal to "mark, learn and inwardly digest". I seem to recall – it was a little while ago – that you mentioned that your Quiet Times were becoming mechanical and dry and what did I think. I am so sorry to have forgotten this until now. Please forgive me. Life for me would be much easier if only I could remember that I forget!

As with what I wrote about Scripture, take your time, but make the time to think, pray about and talk over what I've said with friends. Our forbears attached importance to this and they were right to do so. One of their maxims was, "Never see the face of man until you have seen the face of God". That's good advice. Greet the Lord the moment you wake up. I cannot emphasize enough the importance for the follower of Jesus Christ of having a daily Quiet Time. This is needful on a number of counts.

First, because God knows that for us to live as we should, we should daily be nourished by spiritual food as by regular meals. We need to hear God speak and to speak to him day by day. Just as children grow up evidencing some likeness to their parents, the Quiet Time is a significant aid to assist believers to grow up into the likeness of Christ.

Secondly, it is possible, even probable, that as Christians in other parts of the world continue to be harassed and persecuted, some time in the future Christians in the West may undergo similar treatment. Intolerance of God's truth and of those who firmly hold to it may well gather more momentum. There may come a time when your memorised Bible verses are the only Bible you have.

A third reason for a daily time of quiet and nourishment is that believers have always been, in Augustine's phrase, "resident aliens", in C.S. Lewis', "living in enemy-occupied territory" and, as the Bible expresses it, "here, we have no continuing city." We are sojourners or lodgers, pilgrims who have been enlisted in the King's army for life to fight in a battle between truth and falsehood, honesty and dishonesty, purity and impurity and much else, and our discharge comes only when the Commander himself says personally to each one of his troops, "Well done, good and faithful servant." The Christian soldier must daily buckle on the armour that God has provided by which faith is fortified, convictions confirmed, victories won and holiness cultivated. And here can be seen what is the over-arching purpose: for the anxious children to be drawn nearer to their father and for the father glad to draw near to his children. This surely is its pre-eminent purpose and satisfaction.

It is not always possible to have a *quiet* time. I recall countless instances when flying or in a train, the time has been noisy, perfunctory and unsatisfactory. But for me it was important to be self-disciplined and I knew that the Lord was listening, not simply hearing but listening. Keeping the lines open consists of feeding on the Scriptures and speaking to the Author. Countless passages refer to the necessity for both. Look up Hebrews 4:12–13 and at a sitting read Psalm 119 *aloud*. It is the longest prayer in the Bible and thrills me every time I read it! For young Christians and Christians young in the faith, an ordered plan or scheme to help them find their way through the unity and diversity to be found in sixty-six books, is advisable. There are some helpful Bible-based notes one can read. If you think you're floundering, use a Bible-believing commentary.

As one grows older, under the leadership of the Spirit, one can move around the Bible with continuing humility and more confidence. Understand that you are not only reading words on a page. You are *feeding*, being nourished on the bread of life. God speaking to you in his words is as real as your speaking to God in your words. Ask the Lord to "open (your) eyes that (you) may perceive wondrous things." Make no mistake: in his words, God is speaking directly to *you*, Richard. And one thing that helps to bring home the reality of that is to read aloud. One is more actively involved. You can then place your own emphases or pauses. Before you end the time, make sure you have got hold of something from the reading on which to hold during the day.

One useful approach to prayer is a time-honoured mnemonic ACTS: Adoration, Confession, Thanksgiving, Supplication, pleading for oneself and others. At its simplest, prayer is talking to God. Why not turn some of what you've been feeding on into prayer? Is there encouragement, a warning, something at which to marvel, something for which to say, 'Thank you'? Remember that our father "is more ready to hear than we to pray." And at some point, I think one definitely needs to make a list of people for whom and causes and organizations for which to pray, and that will keep growing! I have prayed in planes, trains, shops and lavatories. I could tell you some stories of the many different places and countries where I've had my Quiet Time! Yet wherever one is, what a joy and relief it is to know that, as the poet William Blake wrote, "I'm in God's presence night and day / And he never takes his face away."

Let me here hasten to say that one should not feel troubled and have guilt feelings if for good reasons from time to time one misses a Quiet Time. Like most routines, it can become mechanical, monotonous. Occasionally, does your time spent in a Quiet Time falter? Do you begin to tire? You don't feel like it. You feel dry, uninterested. Prayer deteriorates into prayerless words. From time to time, these same things have affected and continue to affect me. At such times we really fallen frail folk should not listen to ourselves. As the saying goes, "Listeners never hear good of themselves." We should, like David in the Psalms, *talk* to ourselves, remind ourselves who we are before God and thankfully get on with it! It often helps me on these occasions to sing or recite a verse or two from some of the hymns that I cherish for their spiritual depth. I said something about this in an earlier letter. Try changing place and time or have different Bible notes. Ask your friends how they deal with these matters.

Older and younger followers of Christ ask me if, as I get older, living Christianly becomes easier. I answer always, "No". But, certainly in my own experience, the Scriptures are richer, prayer more natural and frequent, the Holy Spirit seems closer and my eternal home is nearer. So keep going and it will be the same for you. Don't starve yourself. You need your breakfast whether you actually enjoy it or not! Take yourself in hand, refuse to let Satan discourage you and refuse to yield to the fickleness of feelings. Talk honestly to the Lord about it, asking him to help you pull yourself out of the ditch. Look up Psalm 40:1–2, say it aloud and thank the Lord that it's true. I am told by a friend that when a hawk is being trained, like a horse it needs to be broken in. This process it dislikes and will not behave itself; it 'bates'. Then it will not eat. Should that continue, its wing feathers, which determine its wing-span, will not grow. But it can recover and continue to grow by careful feeding and exercise.

At the end of each day, I've had enough and I'm tired! So I read a few verses from Scripture and try to slip into sleep on one of them but not before I've tried to review the day, confessed this and given thanks for that.

In closing, maybe you will appreciate, even emulate this. For more years than I can remember, the moment I wake up I say aloud, 'Lord, thank you for the mercies of the past night and for having brought me safely to the beginning of this new day, wherein "my times (every eventuality) are in your hands."' It is always a *new* day, a day I haven't had before and a day I shan't have again. But I do not forget that there are many suffering souls for whom it is, sadly, just another day. Several cups of strong tea followed by a Quiet Time get me off to a good start. Like the great Dr Johnson, I am "a hardened and shameless tea drinker"!

Every good wish

Donald

PS.   A helpful little book on this subject is *Time Well Spent* by Colin Webster.

FAITH

Dear Richard,

If I may, when next writing I'd like to say something about Doubt. But let me first offer some thoughts on Faith which from the CU card, I see, is shortly to be the subject of a Bible study so I hope this may help you.

As you know, in most important matters one needs first to know the history of that matter as far as appears necessary, in order to arrive at a correct or reasonable conclusion. Thus on matters concerning Christian thought or living we should automatically look to the Scriptures. When we do that, we are struck by the primary fact that the God of the Bible is not only infinite and eternal but also personal. To put it another way, because God is a person, he has a character. And that has enormous consequences because it transpires that the nature of the character of God is the ultimate fact in all matters of faith and belief. As a young believer I began to discover, as I think I have said before, that when I am sure about *that*, I am sure about everything else. And one really important thing of which one needs to be sure is the fact of faith, of certainty, on the basis of the character of God.

Faith is like a rainbow which arches over and embraces each aspect of Christian belief and living. Scripture speaks of faith as "the title-deed of things we hope for, the proof of things we do not see and the conviction of their reality"; "the world which we can see has come into being through principles which are invisible." My faith, your faith in the God of the Bible is utterly dependent on God's faithfulness, an attribute of his character. Faith may be compared also with an apple. There is no apple without first an apple tree. Similarly, my faith cannot exist without his faithfulness. God has a character and one attribute is his unswerving faithfulness to you and me. You and I are first saved and then kept, not by the strength of our faith but by the object:

faith in Christ and nothing else. That means leaning the entire personality on God in absolute trust and confidence in his goodness, power and wisdom. That is faith. Exercising it is like sinking into an armchair that I am confident will take my weight. Life in union with Christ begins with a God-given gift to the seeking soul: faith. But it does not end with faith. As I've said, the object of genuine faith is, as it were, outside itself: God's faithfulness. Let me stress this: life in union and in communion with Christ continues with *my* faith in God and *his* faithfulness to me.

Today, such statements may be thought verging on the lunatic. From the eigthteenth century Enlightenment* to post-modernism, any 'belief system' is disdained – unless it is Post-modern. Faith is regarded as an anachronism, something akin to superstition. Some people will use the word when boarding a plane; they have faith in the plane arriving safely at its destination. But that has nothing to do with faith. What they are doing is invoking the Law of Mathematical Probability. It is more reasonable to say to a person, "I have faith in you," meaning: 'I believe in you, trust you.'

Biblical faith, according to the theologian Alastair McGrath, "is the ability to see God's presence and activity both in the world and in my own experience. It's a willingness to find God where he's promised to be." That is hard to do sometimes yet Luther's statement about Abraham states the truth: "He closed his eyes and hid himself in the darkness of faith and found eternal light in its midst." "*The darkness of faith*" – what a magnificent paradox!

An experience of mine parallels this and may be helpful. After God had made it clear to me that I should resign my housemastership at St Lawrence College in 1969, I made the

---

*Among many Christians, the Enlightenment is almost always denigrated on account of the individualistic tendencies it espoused of contempt for tradition and authority. No good purpose is served by denying that. Yet it did succeed in putting many Christians on their mettle and ultimately in helping to sharpen evangelical witness.

necessary preparations to leave England – for how long, I did not know – and to work at L'Abri Fellowship, an international Christian study centre in Switzerland. My car on the ferry from Dover to Calais had become little less than a packed removal van and leaving it with all the other cars in the hold, I made my way up to the deck. But, to my surprise, my heart was heavy. Unexpectedly, I was assaulted by doubts and questions. A menacing wave of panic wrapped itself around me. Gripping the rail, I watched the distance widening between me and the white cliffs of Dover. Then an announcement over the PA requested me to go to the Purser's office where I was handed a radio message from my brother and his wife wishing me *bon voyage* and every happiness and success. This expression of affection and concern overcame me with gratitude and tears, especially because I felt they didn't understand why I had left the school and was about to join what they not unreasonably imagined to be a hippy commune in the Alps! I cried out to the Lord. Within moments, his strong arm was wrapped around me. I was suffused with inner peace and thankfulness which remained for the rest of the journey to Switzerland. Not again did darkness shroud me. Never again, even fleetingly, have I lost faith in God's faithfulness.

You too may undergo severe trials like many other believers, and have frightening experiences. Consider Job in these respects. He held fast to God throughout some appalling physical experiences, continuing to believe and obey, and God brought him through them. Remember that today there are an estimated two hundred million believers in different parts of the world who are undergoing persecution and unimaginable hardship only because they are Christians. Go on trusting God; never mind the hardship. Your faith in his faithfulness may bring loss, prejudice and contempt. At such times, ask yourself the probing question: *what is my faith worth to me in this situation?* Go on believing in God, as Abraham did, who is not playing games with you. Remind yourself that there's no going back; that you belong to Christ and he has promised that he will see you safely through to the end.

What matters therefore is not the greatness of your faith but the greatness of God. Faith is a fact, not a fancy. It can be understood. It can be defined. It is not nodding one's head to a series of propositions. It is closely following Jesus. Yet it is not something that acts automatically. As Martyn Lloyd-Jones expresses it, "Some people seem to think that faith is like a thermostat on a heating apparatus .... if the temperature rises, the thermostat brings it down. If the temperature lowers, the thermostat sends it up. You do nothing about it. It acts automatically." That is not so. In the Bible, obedience, hope and faith are connected concepts and activities. Faith is not to be thought of as a passive attribute. An attribute of faith is certainty but *you have to bring it into operation* by calling out to the Lord. When temptations and testings slip in and difficulties and down-castings demand admittance, seize the covering shield of faith, thus making it operative and energizing as you call upon God's help to see you through each situation.

The apostle James writes in his letter that faith by itself is inoperative, dead. A car fails to fulfil its function unless it is driven. By good deeds and obedient actions, faith shows that it is real, active and productive. For example, if you pray about how to use a Gap year perhaps with Careforce in a downtrodden, deprived area in Britain or somewhere in The Third World, easing ignorance and hunger, you are exercising faith, declaring that it is a reality. Faithfulness in anything, especially a little thing, is a great thing.

By the same token, having faith is not only a personal, private matter. It's not wrapping an overcoat round me for warmth. It is to be activated, made alert, for example while you're discussing with friends or find yourself in a tricky spot. As well as 'private' conviction, faith is what has been called 'public' truth. You and I declare and seek to show that Christians can and do stand publicly for the truth of the gospel in today's society. Generally speaking, today's churches are not connecting with people outside them anymore. The life of faith you and I lead can powerfully be used by God to lead others to know about him.

Today, I don't feel quite up to the mark as I usually do. Perhaps Ogden Nash is right: "A mighty creature is the germ, though smaller than the pachyderm. / His customary dwelling place, is deep within the human race. / His childish pride he often pleases, by giving people strange diseases. / Do you, my poppet, feel infirm? You probably contain a germ!"

Best wishes

Donald

DOUBT

Dear Richard,

No, I'm thankful to report that I didn't have a germ and seem OK again!

I thought that a letter about a subject of which I have some knowledge but no experience might surprise you. I am referring to Doubt, something that suddenly or slowly envelops some folk like the feeble light from a failing torch that leaves one in the dark. For some time, I have been – and still am – anxious about certain matters at large that are developing. Two small examples: sometimes in evangelism there is the practice of preaching Christ and seldom referring to God; in preaching, the practice of continually using the word 'story', e.g. 'the story' of Elijah and the prophets of Baal or 'the story' of Jesus feeding 5000 people, because to most unbelievers listening or reading, that word means fiction, fantasy, myth. I am anxious too whether believers are making significant intellectual dents in the carapace of post-modernism. I have such anxieties. But I have never had any doubts – questions yes, but not doubts – about anything to do with the Scriptures or its outworkings day by day. I am surprised at this and thankful for it, for numbers of believers undergo times of doubt.

Today's intellectual climate has no belief in any certainties, Christian or otherwise. Its hopes are that science will continue to provide the key for solving some present and future problems. But for many people the intellectual climate implicitly assumes doubt and, for most people, sceptical unbelief. No brittle scepticism should afflict a follower of Jesus Christ. But Doubt may. In writing on this subject, I warmly recommend to any troubled person the writer Os Guinness' book *God in the Dark,* and from it summarise several points.

At one time or another, Christians may be afflicted by Doubt. We don't doubt because we're Christians but because we're human.

There is nothing unusual or sinful in having doubts. One's salvation is not threatened. God is unchangeable in his faithfulness to his promises. Doubt is not the same as unbelief. Neither is it unbelief's opposite. Faith is. Doubt is not a fixed choice, only an uncertainty. It is being in two minds about someone or something. Those who have faith may also have doubts. Peter and Thomas had both and Jesus gently reproved them. But he did not say that they had lost their faith. We have to reckon with the fact that an uncertain or weak faith can lead to doubt and also that there are honest intellectual and irrational doubts as well as doubts generated by strong emotions.

Martyn Lloyd-Jones has observed that immoral behaviour or intellectual scepticism also can push towards doubt. Often when we sin, we condemn ourselves and that too may lead to doubt. Yet, when confessing the sin and pleading for forgiveness, doubt disappears. A further reason for doubt, as Lloyd-Jones observes, is a misunderstanding of the nature of faith: ".... faith is something active .... that must be applied .... if we realize that faith appropriates, lays hold upon, we will get rid of our doubts and then faith will become strong." Never let doubts shove certainties aside. When you're unsure, deliberately stand on the things of which you are sure, staying there until it's safe to move.From time to time, I've tramped across Dartmoor and every so often one encounters a bog. One immediately stops and looks for a way round or a way through.

There is an episode in the preacher John Bunyan's *The Pilgrim's Progress* when Christian and Hopeful, on their journey to the Celestial City, take a short cut across a meadow in order to avoid a stony path. But in a few minutes, night envelops them and a storm breaks. Yet they plod on and through the rain a castle begins to take shape. They are observed and a giant emerging from the castle grasps and then flings them into a dungeon. They realize that they are imprisoned in Doubting Castle, the home of Giant Despair who shows them the skeletons of other pilgrims who have trespassed on his property. They wonder if they will ever escape. Christian then remembers that he has a key in his pocket named Promise and by using it, they escape. They are free. What a simple, superb truth! Forgetting feelings and focusing on facts – on God and his promises – they overcome Doubt, the small, by looking away to God, the great.

The biblical doctrine of Assurance has something to say about this too. We can have faith without having an assurance of faith, and when temptation slips in and if we slide into sin, we may wonder whether we really are in union with our Saviour. True, my salvation is secure throughout this life and eternity. My head knows that – but sometimes my heart doesn't. As Martyn Lloyd-Jones points out, true assurance includes both and has several solid evidences. The first is that God's word clearly assures us of Assurance: if we believe, we do have eternal life. Secondly, we begin to love our fellow Christians. Then there is wanting to obey God's commandments and follow Christ. Fourthly, the Holy Spirit is living within us. Also, we gradually become more sensitive to sin and loathe it. Sixthly, we desire more knowledge of God and the things belonging to God. Seventhly, there is evidence of the fruits of the Spirit and a longing for holiness. Eighthly, there is humility. Finally, from time to time there is an examination of the state of our life. What glorious assurances, Richard! We keep on holding on to *his faithfulness to us*, not our faith in him. We are to keep on pushing away the spotlight from ourselves and swivelling it on to *God*. Write this out and stick it on a wall where you can see and say it: "Let me no more my comfort draw / from my frail hold of Thee. / In this alone rejoice with awe: / thy mighty grasp of me".

All good wishes

Donald

FRAILTY & FOOLISHNESS: THE TABLES TURNED

Dear Richard,

Some time ago, I came across the following two extracts and think you may find them, as used to be said, 'instructive'.

This is the first. "Union with Christ imparts an inner elevation, comfort in affliction, tranquil reliance, and a heart which opens itself to everything noble and great, not for the sake of ambition or desire for fame, but for the sake of Christ. Union with Christ produces a joy which the Epicurean seeks in vain in his shallow philosophy, which the deeper thinker vainly pursues in the most hidden depths of knowledge. It is a joy known only to the simple and childlike heart, united with Christ and through Him with God, a joy which elevates life and makes it more beautiful."

Here's the second. "You know, I think, that I believe in no religion. There is absolutely no proof for any of them, and from a philosophical standpoint Christianity is not even the best. All religions, that is, all mythologies to give them their proper name, are merely man's own invention – Christ as much as Loki. Primitive man found himself surrounded by all sorts of terrible things he didn't understand..... Thus religion, that is to say, mythology, grew up. Often, too, great men were regarded as gods after their death – such as Heracles or Odin: thus after the death of a Hebrew philosopher Yeshua (whose name we have corrupted into Jesus) became regarded as a god, a cult sprang up, which was afterwards connected with the ancient Hebrew Jahweh-worship, and so Christianity came into being – one mythology among many..... Of course, mind you, I am not laying down as a certainty that there is nothing outside the material world: considering the discoveries that are always being made, this would be foolish. Anything *may* exist."

There is no prize for guessing. But would you hazard a guess who wrote each of them, both written when they were still in their teens?

The Marxist Karl Marx wrote the first, the scholar C.S. Lewis the second.

What happened to change the thinking and then, inevitably, the direction of the lives of those two young men? They had the assurance, even the arrogance that many of us have in our teens and early twenties. They also appear at the time profoundly to have believed in what they said. So what happened to bring about a total denial and reversal of what they had believed?

I know next to nothing about Marx's life and one would need to investigate what caused him to renounce his youthful, joyous convictions. As for Lewis, his books give us all the information we need to know why he reversed his youthful atheist or agnostic convictions.

There may be more to say about this but what can certainly be said is that, as for most human beings, the ability freely to make choices was freely made. Moreover, all choices inevitably have consequences, in time and in eternity. Your choice, Richard, has been to give your life to Christ and to go on so doing. Yet, as Scripture repeatedly warns us and illustrates, for example, Judas' treachery and Peter's attitude at Jesus' trial, it is possible to repudiate and deny him and the truth. Recall that verse in I Corinthians: 'Don't be naive and self-confident. You're not exempt. You could fall flat on your face as easily as anyone else. Forget about self-confidence. It's useless. Cultivate God-confidence. He'll never let you down nor be pushed past your limit. And get out of unhelpful company as fast as you can!' (The Message)

Today is one of those crisp, crackling-with-frost days. As I've said, I love all the weathers God sends and the daily sightings of part of his creation for, as the poet W. H. Davies asks, "What is this life if, full of care / We have no time to stand and stare?"

Best wishes

Donald

TEMPTATION

Dear Richard,

Thanks so much for phoning. I agree with you that Marx's faith seems sincere but too emotional whereas Lewis' doubt, or unbelief, seems juvenile but pardonable arrogance. But your chief point warmed my heart: "He who thinks he stands should take care in case he falls", while he who does not believe should pray, "Lord, I believe. Help my unbelief". Our review makes a suitable introduction to this letter, don't you think?

Yesterday, I found myself thinking about temptation and wondering whether it existed any more. More likely, it has joined the noble army of recently martyred words, which may be traced back to the end of World War II, such as sin, guilt, shame, duty, purity, sanctity, diligence, sportsmanship, self–respect, self–discipline, self–control, decency, chastity, nobility, modesty, womanliness, manliness, courtesy, honour, truth, trust, truthfulness, each burnt or burning at the stake of relativism. Not only do unused words gradually become disused or discarded words. What they mean or represent assumes little or no importance or, in practice, actually cease to exist. I would say that of the permissive society since the 1960s, 'temptation' along with those other words has not only fallen into disuse but may no longer have meaning or significance for the average person. That may apply, too, to some believers. If so, that is a serious matter and would reveal an inadequate view of sin as well as giving a wrong testimony to others. No Christian can afford to take temptation lightly – when it means temptation to evil – any more than sin and Satan may be taken lightly. Temptation of this kind is not a trapeze on which I test my ability to overcome it. That is to do despite to the Saviour.

Temptation is not only enticement to evil, something seductive or alluring. It is that: a tussle for the mastery between the best and the worst parts of our nature. But it includes also the process of testing, of proving . The biblical idea leans more in the latter direction: human beings test their fellows; men and women audaciously test God; God tests his people and Satan tests God's people. We test ourselves prior to receiving the Lord's Supper. Temptations or testings come both from God and Satan, the latter being God's instrument as well as his enemy. But temptation is not the same as sin. Similar to conscience, temptation is the orange, not the red traffic light.

Sometimes it is God who is testing different aspects of our Christian character, proving us in temptation. My character is being hammered out on the anvil of temptation. It is being forged in conflict and each time evil is faced and conquered, then faith is fortified and the struggle is rendered easier next time. More often than not, it is Satan who works unceasingly to try to cancel the believer's allegiance to Jesus Christ by manipulating circumstances "within the limits that God allows him." He works eagerly to organize our lives. In some way, he is able to insinuate himself, to prise open the mind and tease the temperament.

If I were writing a reference for Satan, I would unhesitatingly recommend him for his unfailing talent for being three things: venomous, devious and assiduous. He is brilliant too in promoting personal, social and cosmic evil of all kinds. Allied to these effectively employed gifts is a genius for spindoctoring both accusation and confusion in the minds of his Adversary's bewildered victims. In this too, he is an unparalleled success.

In the Scriptures, Satan is seen as a master of disguises, an actor who "in his time plays many parts": Lucifer, serpent, a liar and the father of lies, god of this world, angel of light, prince of the power of the air, ruler of this present darkness, roaring lion, dragon, accuser of the brethren, devil, each name describing a characteristic of his nature and purpose. That purpose has always been inflexible: to drive, and keep on driving, a wedge between the follower of Jesus Christ and God's grace. By the same token, he foments deepening intellectual confusion and ever-widening moral turpitude at all levels of society and in all countries.

Temptation is one of the hammers he uses. It comes at any time in different forms. To me, it comes invariably when I'm feeling tired like Esau, or light-headed like Herod, or depressed like Peter. A slight thing then can make me hot, hasty and horrible, particularly when I'm confronted by some inanimate object that doggedly insists on its right to have a life of its own! Then I become a bundle of contradictions. The poet Gerard Manley Hopkins' line comes to mind: "O thou Lord of life, send my roots rain!"

I'm appalled at the mean-spirited nastiness that is sometimes me. I cry out to the Lord for help and keep on crying out until the enemy has retreated. "Look away to Jesus....." But, as I've said, time and again I surrender and then feel wretched until I've repented and know I'm forgiven.

Temptation seems to have four stages: a thought, a look or a second thought, a fascination, a fall. If that surging advance is to be stopped, it must be at the first stage. The reformer Martin Luther records that on one occasion when he was undergoing prolonged temptation, in imagination he saw a black dog (which represented the devil) lying on his bed which he at once seized and threw out of the window. Is not the first stage, 'at once', the vital decision? "Thanks be to God who has given us the victory through our Lord Jesus Christ".

This 'at once' applies in other ways. For example, I have a friend who, addicted to pornography, hoarded porn magazines. When he became a believer, he burned them all. I know of a man, addicted to alcohol, who on his way home each evening after work would generously imbibe at his local pub. After becoming a follower of Jesus Christ, he permanently changed his route home. Both these people wanted to be free from sin so they put their faith to work, acted at once and have continued – as did temptation – to witness to God's rescuing power through Christ. They were gripped by the truth that Christ has given us a life of freedom. Of course, that does not mean that believers have freedom to sin. Rather does it mean the freedom *not* to sin! When we call for help, we can be freed to do the will of God.

When in August 1914 the Great War began, the British Government persuaded itself and the nation that it would be over by the end of the year. This was not a firm promise but a foolish boast because it was believed that the Royal Navy would impose a successful blockade on German ports and bring that nation to its knees. But drawing on years of battle experience in Egypt, Field Marshal Lord Kitchener told the Cabinet that the War would last "at least three years or for the duration. And the war will be won only by the last million men whom Great Britain can raise, train, equip and hurl into battle". We should not deceive ourselves. Temptation is never in remission. God's beneficent testing and Satan's malevolent tempting will continue until, to quote John Bunyan's noble words, the trumpets sound for us on the other side. Skirmishing will persist but the victory has been won and followers of Jesus Christ gratefully call upon the resources of his victory when "the enemy surges in like a flood, for the spirt of the Lord *shall* lift up a standard against him."

There's no sign of Spring yet. In fact, we had a few inches of snow and I read aloud – always aloud! – a couple of 'snow' poems, Robert Bridges' *London Snow* and Francis Thompson's *To a Snowflake*. Have a look at them – but say them aloud!

Every good wish

Donald

PS. Please remember me warmly to your parents. Thank you. I wonder if your father has been able to find a job?

ANOTHER BRIEF NOTE

Dear Richard,

Thank you for ringing me about the spot of trouble you got into. I'm not minimising the foolishness nor the possible consequences of what you did by calling it 'a spot' of trouble. I mean that it was not sinful although, as you said, it was shaming. Your voice told me that you feel bad about it, unworthy and I feel for you in this. You could have kept quiet about it but chose to discuss it. I've always respected you but that I admire.

But it's time for you to put this behind you, where you can't see it. As I've said before, don't let the past put a brake on the present. Talk to the Lord about it and repent, pleading for his strength to keep and protect you and your girl-friend. Heavy petting is perilously close to having sex but it's not the same thing. Of course it's pleasurable and is usually the prelude to going the whole way.

The majority of people nowadays chiefly seem to value material success and instant gratification. Your generation is particularly susceptible to peer pressure in every area in which it's possible to have peer pressure! Your contemporaries and their mentors almost demand conformity to today's secular beliefs and lifestyles. Most of them are not merely indifferent to Christian thinking but are actively hostile and I think will become more so. 'No problem, everybody does it' is said to apply to each potential young adult situation. Add hormones and every door is open.

God created sex but big business and film studios continue to make vast fortunes out of it. Each day, TV, magazines, advertising hoardings and the way many women dress create temptaion and arouse desire. It's worth spending time reading and praying through Tony Payne and Philip Jensen's little book *Pure Sex*.

Before you put this behind you once and for all, learn from it Richard. You doubtless know why it happened. But *how* did it happen? *How* did you get yourselves into that situation? Honestly face up to dealing with *that* to prevent it happening again. But don't torture yourself. Be sure also why sex before marriage is displeasing to God and harmful to you.

It has been said that sex is a language with which we communicate love. By love should be meant that which wants permanent commitment, not shabby one-night-stands. Why is this? Because people are made in God's image and are therefore valuable. So to use sex for less than this is to undervalue it and the person with whom one is in a relationship. As a friend of mine said, "Love is a conversation, not a competition". Each person should be upholding the other's God-given value.

Knowing you, you'll take this seriously but not crushingly. Why not also use a few verses from Scripture when talking with the Lord about it? Psalm 40:1–3, Ephesians 1: 7 and Psalm 51 fit the bill. Don't lie in a muddy puddle, moaning away. You've been in a skirmish, not lost a war. Rejoice in and give thanks for his forgiveness. Get up and go on!

All good wishes

Donald

GUIDANCE

Dear Richard,

Some years ago, the media carried an account of the minister of a church who had planned to swim the English Channel but was compelled to turn back after swimming a short distance. When asked why he was making the attempt, he had replied simply, "The thought came from the Lord." Certainly God can choose out of the blue to guide a person. But that good man had overlooked several necessary principles which God has given which normally apply to guidance.

The Bible reveals numerous examples of God's guidance to individuals. Here are a few: through Moses and Joshua he spoke to the Israelites. He addressed Abraham, Elijah, Solomon and Hezekiah. In the Psalms and in the New Testament, he promises to guide his people. His purposes and promises for his people remain unchanged. Because God cannot lie, does not break his promises, never lets us go, never lets us down, does not play games with us, we can trust him. Because he loves us, he wants the best for us. Sometimes we think we know what is best for us. William Carey wanted to go as a missionary to Polynesia. God sent him to India. David Livingstone wanted to go to China. God sent him to Africa. Let the Lord have his way. He guides us – if we are willing – in great and in small matters. He guides our common sense.

When I kept failing a Mathematics examination for entry to university, I pleaded for guidance. He gave it, I persisted and was admitted. When the founders of L'Abri Fellowship, Francis and Edith Schaeffer, needed a home in Switzerland and earnestly prayed for it, God led them to the right châlet. To purchase it, he provided the actual amount of money on the last permissible day! Throughout my life as a believer, in each eventuality when I have been aware of my smallness and helplessness, the Holy Spirit has prompted me to plead for the Lord's guidance and to thank him for his faithfulness. "I steadier step when I recall / that though I slip, you do not fall."

What principles has God given? First, your mind and heart have to be united in the deliberate intention to have no will of your own in the matter. That is a hard saying. It is sometimes difficult to accept and we rebel. But it is fundamental. There has to be total trust in his wisdom and in his love for you. There has to be a wholehearted willingness to be led and then to obey. Plead with him to speak and to keep on speaking through Scripture; the Spirit and the Word will be combined. Ask him to speak too through any other means he chooses. Ask him to give you a trusting, restful spirit. Talk to him about the matter and persevere in praying. Use your common-sense. Take circumstances into account. You may ask the advice of friends although sometimes conflicting views may confuse you.

But this is the crucial principle: to God your Father you vow – which is no less significant but is deeper than a promise because it is a solemn resolve, a sacred undertaking – that you want to know and will do his will, "nothing more, nothing less, nothing else – at any cost". And you persevere and quietly go on persevering in your pleading for clear reflection and decision. For example, you have been asked to join a student party, all of whom are unbelievers, going winter sporting. Your name has been put forward for committee membership of the Student Union at the same time as having been invited to be the CU rep. in your hall. You are wondering whether you are studying the right subject and can see no alternative subject. Os Guinness is helpful here: "We do not trust God because he guides us. We trust him and are then guided. Faith may be in the dark about guidance but is never in the dark about God. What he may be doing may be a mystery. But who God is, is not." Trust him, talk to him. He loves you and he *will* lead you. Even if you make a wrong decision, as the writer Peter Lewis says, "he is still sovereign and able to fit it into his plan for our lives, over-ruling it for good and moving us towards his prepared path."

Contrast a biblical, quietly confident approach with the well-meant but naive statement of that dear man who attempted a Channel crossing. Or compare a biblical approach with that of a student who arrived at Swiss L'Abri. This earnest, confused young man, when asked what he had in mind to study replied, "Nothing. God has called me to be a missionary." In answer to my asking to what country he thought God was leading him and did he know the language of the people, to the first question he answered, "God will show me," to the second, "No". We talked but to little purpose. Sadly, he left the following day. Again, God can choose so to prepare and equip a person, for example, Moses, but such appointments appear to be rare.

Both the above approaches unhappily reveal a deficiency of Scriptural understanding and of the application that follows such understanding, not to speak of the abdication of common-sense. So do the beliefs and practices of some Christians today who are known to seek God's guidance through "pictures in the mind". There are those who concentrate on the flame of a candle. Like Buddhists, others try to empty their minds. Still others assert that "God has told me" such and such. And indeed, God may have done but such folk should find confirmation for that assertion. Let me carefully say that these practices cannot possibly be right for any follower of Jesus Christ. They are done as though the Scriptures did not exist. They are believed as though there was no Holy Spirit. They are practised as though prayer had no purpose. Moreover, they are potentially dangerous practices, dipping one's toes into the pool of the occult.

But does the living God speak through his written word? Is he my father? Am I his child? All his promises resound with the splendour of trumpets: Yes! And when I am ready to make a decision, I act upon it, go ahead in this or that direction yet still pleading with the Lord to bless or to block my being acted–upon decision. I prayerfully ponder Luther's comment; he is speaking

particularly of the Psalms and it applies to all of Scripture: "...
we can find counsel and comfort nowhere else and this alone is
the golden art: to cling to God's Word and promise, *to make
judgments on the basis of this word* (my italics) and not on the
basis of the feelings of the heart. Then help and comfort will
surely follow". How true, as I have found!

Remember your vow, Richard. The more you trust yourself to
him, the more he will reveal to you what he knows you need.
"Your way, not mine, O Lord, however dark it be .... choose you
the path for me".

It's time for tea and toast! I read recently that as a young man,
the naturalist Charles Darwin learned what he considered to be
the golden rule for saving time: taking care of the minutes. Wise
man!

All good wishes

Donald

PS.   Your friend next door: may I ask if you have been able to
have a worthwhile conversation?

UNCOVERING YOUR GIFTS

Dear Richard,

When you kindly asked me to write about some of the concerns I have for students and other young Christians, I had not reckoned on there being so many! I shall continue to do my best and hope that the result will not be like the experience I had at an American university when noticing a label on the electric hand-dryer in the Men's Room which read, "If you wish to listen to one of the Dean's lectures, press this button!" I hope that you will always remember that I am not writing from some lofty spiritual eminence. Rather is it that through the years under God I have acquired some knowledge, a modicum of wisdom and a certain amount of experience – which is why I'm a little further along the King's highway than you are. Yet it's always Ps. 115: 1.

The lives of those who have gone ahead remind us that we too are on that mighty river of History that flows through the centuries. We are not, as sometimes appears to be, marooned in the twenty-first-century. We are on the same voyage as the biblical writers, first century Christians, the heroes and heroines named in Hebrews 11 along with the people of God through the running centuries to our own day. We each have different gifts, we each have different callings. But we are all in the same boat, all sailing in the same direction. Talking about boats reminds me of how much you enjoy rowing. Did you know that for each crew member in the Oxford and Cambridge Boat Race, the rowing is equivalent to lifting 56 lbs from feet to neck 34 times a minute for 20 minutes? Isn't that something?

But to the subject of this letter: gifts. None of what I want to say undervalues God's gracious and generous provision of a Saviour and in addition, his gifts of common grace to believers and unbelievers alike and to animals and vegetation. To believers, he gives the Holy Spirit as Comforter and as the co-ordinator of all the gifts that are to be used to bring praise to him, blessing to others and benefit to ourselves.

A further donation of which we are not usually aware until some time has elapsed, is one of the special gifts that are listed in Paul's first letter to the Corinthians. None of these is to be confused with those of which I am here speaking: through parents and God's personal, individual gifts of character and creativity to each human being. It is not surprising to find that in Greek, 'gifts' and 'grace' have the same root meaning. God has given each of us certain gifts and withheld other gifts. Those he has given you are the right ones and in the right proportion for you. Our gifts mark us out as separate, significant individuals with unique contributions to make. As the parable of the talents indicates, these gifts of character and creativity are to be employed, not hoarded. Without false modesty, make an inventory. Did you know you had all these gifts? Are you using them? Incidentally, realizing what one's gifts are can be helpful when thinking about a career. The creative gifts require the character gifts for their full implementation. God is such a *generous* giver!

Yet I would add a caution. It sometimes happens that the gifts to some young people indicate, say, a possible career in film, journalism or music. But perhaps from their parents or from well-meaning but short-sighted Christian folk, the impression is received that to do such work is not really the best way to serve God. "Why don't you get a proper job? Are there not more fulfilling professions? Have you considered part or 'full-time' ministry?" Let me gently say that one should not fulfil one's parents' dreams or submit to peer or job pressure unless one is entirely at ease about it. What matters most is not others' pressure from outside but your passion from inside. You need your gifts to be affirmed and given an opportunity to be tested. I recall several occasions when I have sought not to persuade but to dissuade students from thinking of entering 'the ministry' or for that matter applying to university, unless as it were, God seizes them by the scruff of the neck and propels them into it. Uncover your gifts, prayerfully offer them back to God, examine them for they have a crucial rôle in the guidance you also need.

The story is told of a parish priest in a German village during the Middle Ages who encouraged his congregation to bring and place round the altar evidence of the creative gifts God had given them. So the wheel-wright brought an engraved new wheel, a housewife placed a pie made from her own new recipe. Living in the village was a juggler who despairingly bemoaned his lack of gifts. When Sunday came, the crowded chancel displayed the evidence of much creativity. But just as the service was about to begin, the juggler walked the length of the church to the altar – juggling to the glory of God! There's no such thing as a gift that is insignificant or unusable.

It's again time for my walk which is not only for exercise. Henry Ford remarked that exercise, just like history, is 'bunk': "If you are healthy, you don't need it. If you are sick, you shouldn't take it". But surely, to remain healthy, you do need it! I am so grateful to God for good health and strength, for work still to do and willingness to do it. Occasionally on my walk and more so when driving, I find dead animals on the road, killed by speeding cars and the animals' own unfamiliarity with them. I can't bear to see them broken and exposed like that and whenever possible, stop and place them on the verge or in a ditch. Sentimental? No. True sentiment? I think so.

Every good wish

Donald

DEEDS NOT WORDS

Dear Richard,

As regards their length, I fear that some of my letters are beginning to resemble those 18th century writers like Lord Chesterfield and Horace Walpole. As regards their content, mine are different. Chesterfield's *Letters to his Son* and *Letters to his Godson*, none of which was intended for publication contain, except in certain particulars, wise advice but little encouragement to what might be called lofty living. Most such letters then breathed more than a whiff of the Enlightenment culture. But you would, I think, approve of W.H. Auden's *Epistle to a Godson* and also *Letters of Francis A. Schaeffer* edited by Lane T. Dennis. *Letters to Malcolm* by C.S. Lewis are also rewarding as are *The Letters of J.R.R. Tolkien.*

Whilst reflecting on the subject of Letters, I came across a passage from the writer Jacques Ellul's *Reason for Being: a meditation on Ecclesiastes,* which is the sort of thing I'd like to have written to you and other student friends. Here's an extract "Remember your Creator during your youth when all possibilities lie open before you and you can offer all your strength intact for his service. The time to remember is not after you have become senile and paralysed! Then it is not too late for your salvation but (it is) too late for you to serve as the presence of God in the midst of the world and the creation. You must take sides earlier, when you can actually make choices, when you have many paths opening at your feet, before the weight of necessity overwhelms you." What wise words!

What you believe about God, human life and history *now* will determine your behaviour when you've left university. 'Now' and 'then' are interdependent. The sharp truth that distils from Ellul's observation is compressed in Jesus' words: "For where your treasure is, there your heart will be also." In other words, what you value and hope for is what you love and long for. Your belief decides your behaviour. "A man is not what he thinks he is but what he *thinks*, he is." And probably for the majority of people, as the novelist Iris Murdoch warns, "at crucial moments of choice most of the business of choosing is already over."

Leaving belief on one side for the moment, the matter of what constitutes Christian behaviour is what should concern you and me. If my generation was too legalistic, yours is far too permissive. The pressure to follow the crowd, especially on Christians young in the faith, is enormous. It's unremitting, as you know. It arises from various secular bases such as the triple momentum of music, movies and magazines; the hero-worship of – I say this gently – unheroic personalities and celebrities; sex and drugs as part of entertainment; the attitude of 'No one's got the right to tell me what to do', coupled with the easy-come, easy-go attitude expressed in the word 'whatever'. These can continue to establish a bridgehead in belief and then behaviour.

Ruthlessly and relentlessly, Satan tries to squeeze us into the world's way of thinking and living. Some Christians' lifestyle seems to be little different from unbelievers for they appear to have become so well-adjusted to the culture that they fit into it without even thinking. Such lifestyle has lovingly to be reproved and if necessary, lovingly condemned. They watch the same TV programmes, read the same magazines, follow the same fashions. God's standards are often obliterated by such choices. In the political world, it is said that it's time to bring an ambassador home when he's learned the language and adopted the customs of the country to which he's been assigned.

The difference lies between those of us who believe that God is there and has truthfully spoken to all and those who do not. Today, to assert the validity and authority of the Bible as speaking truth about God, the cosmos, history and the human condition is probably met with incredulity or with the ultimate dismissal: "So what? Who cares?" Tragically, the iron has entered into so many peoples' souls. When the Bible is disregarded, its ethics are also disregarded. When Christian truth has been bulldozed, Christian morality can find no foothold. In the West for fourteen centuries, the Bible's teaching about behaviour has been a tested and reliable foundation for individual and social behaviour. It is a blue-print for a healthy society.

We make choices about behaviour as we do about everything else. Nowadays, does not the average student make many choices on impulse rather than thought and not guarded even by residual moral beliefs that might somewhat restrain or restrict? As the writer G.K. Chesterton said, "When men cease to believe in God, they do not believe in nothing. They believe in *anything*." This results in 'anything goes,' going with the flow. Where does that leave the follower of Jesus Christ? In some matters, should there be differences between the behaviour of believers and unbelievers? Humanly speaking, a believer is neither *better* than, nor superior to, an unbeliever. Each is made in the image of God, able to think, to feel, to love, to will and to create. But a believer's behaviour should at times be *different*. He or she is on that mighty river that flows through the centuries along with all the people of God. They were steadfast to the end and did not love their lives, even to the point of death. Why not be cheered by reading about them again in Hebrews 11?

The way we believers behave is overwhelmingly important in two ways: it is observable; it makes a difference. We may think it goes unnoticed and has little or no significance. That is not true. Stephen's dying witness was the occasion of Paul's conversion. Luther's testimony at the Diet of Worms was the spark that ignited the Reformation. Dietrich Bonhoeffer's resolution led to the fortifying of German Christians even though he was hanged by the Nazis. Your telling your unbelieving friends, as one of the students from my church did, that dabbling in the occult will have perilous consequences will not, as happened on that occasion, be without good effect. Yet as I have known, it is not easy to speak up for the truth. But when you've done it once, the next time it is easier. The decisive question to be asked every time, as each of the examples above illustrates is: *what is my faith worth to me at this point?* I remember a student friend who was once angrily rebuked by a non-believing fellow student with these words, "Never, ever talk to me about Christianity again." And he hasn't done so. At that point, I consider my friend should have refused the request and carefully explained why. But sad to say, he appears to have been treading spiritual water ever since.

Let me widen this matter. Feeling intimidated by unbelieving friends who resent the claim that Christianity alone is the truth is only part of the problem of presenting the Gospel. Another is that we ourselves may be tempted to suspect that they are right on insisting that 'religious views' not only lack a basis in fact but also are a matter of personal opinion. That was one of the planks in Enlightenment thinking into which postmodernism has hammered the nails of all knowledge as coming ultimately from a rational viewpoint. It is alleged that revelation as the way to know God is not rational knowledge and cannot be compared with science which can show cause and effect. But as the theologian Lesslie Newbigin has shown and the scientist Michael Polanyi before him, Christian faith "is not irrational but represents a wider rationality than that posited by the norms of scientific discovery, because the Gospel opens the question of *purpose* (my italics), which scientific knowing (has) set aside in favour of cause and effect." By 'purpose' is meant the reason for the universe being here and being knowable as well as for humankind being here and needing salvation.

Over a period of 1400 years, we in Britain can summon witnesses to the personal, social and national benefits that the Gospel brings and continues to bring. Let one contemporary example suffice. In South Africa in 1994, it was Christian people on all sides who were instrumental in ensuring a peaceful transition, through the first multi-racial election, from the minority white government to a full democracy.

Linked to a certain fearfulness about making a stand for Christian truth is the approach of many of your contemporaries to making moral judgments on this attitude or that action. This is a thoroughly natural position for a relativist to adopt. The absence of absolutes means that a person has to make up his or her own meanings. Invariably, tolerance triumphs over truth. The classic formula that sanctifies this view seems to be 'There's no right nor wrong. It's a matter of opinion. Who are we to judge?' I say this carefully but there is a certain amount that is poisonous about some aspects of youth culture today and this is an example. If this foolish approach had been applied to Nazism, what would have happened to our country and to Europe? In a court of law, suppose the jury decided to be 'non-judgmental' about murderers or rapists? What would be the consequences in a sporting event if a referee or an umpire refused to make judgments? Without making judgments, that which was achieved individually, socially, nationally because of the effects of the 18th century Evangelical Revival would never have been achieved. Relativism reinforces subjectivism.

Part of Relativism is the New Tolerance which maintains that what is deemed wrong for one person is not necessarily wrong for another. Each person is entitled to have his or her opinion of right or wrong. But this is not tolerance but broadmindedness. Tolerance means a respect for others' beliefs without sharing them, no more, no less. It has nothing to do with being 'enlightened' or 'liberated', sadly, another illustration of the novelist Doestoevesky's observation that 'when God is dead, everything is permitted.'

I plead with you, Richard, do not 'go with the flow'. Cry for the unbeliever, get alongside and *stay* alongside him or her. But keep away from that dirty stream. You have a choice. Continue to turn your back on evil. But do not close your eyes to it. Recall the poet John Milton's sturdy pleading for freedom of the Press in *Areopagitica*,: "He that can apprehend and consider vice with all her wants and seeming pleasures and yet abstain and yet distinguish and yet prefer that which is truly better, he is the true way-faring Christian." Then comes the challenge: "I cannot praise a fugitive and cloistered virtue, unexercised and unbreathed, that never sallies out and sees her adversary but slinks out of the race where that immortal garland is to be run for, not without dust or heat."

It's hard. I know that. I know also that Paul encouraged himself in the Lord (and us), not by saying, "I *must* go on doing all things through Christ who goes on strengthening me" but by saying, "I *can* go on doing all things through Christ who goes on strengthening me." It is not the self-imposed burdensome imperative but the quiet confidence in God's loving faithfulness that steadies and compels.

I'm pleased to know the river was not iced and I would like to hear how the team and you got on in the rowing finals. Writing that puts me in mind of the telegram which read: "Start worrying. Letter to follow!". This is more than enough for one letter.

Best wishes

Donald

FRIENDSHIP AND HARDSHIP

Dear Richard,

Thank you for ringing the other evening. Yes, it would be good to meet to discuss some of the matters we've raised recently and I would much welcome that.

Some time ago, I attempted to review the successive philosophies which have led to post-modernism. The cumulative weight of secularism engendered by these ideas suffocates society but provides believers with many openings for gospel truth. I pointed out also the need for followers of Christ to live in friendship and in fellowship. A sane, loving and Bible-believing church where one is aware that one is part of the world-wide worshipping family of God forms part of that. So does the Christian Union. We need fellowship. In his first letter, the apostle John describes it as a distinguishing mark of Christians. A mark of genuine fellowship is the love that believers have for one another because that is evidence of God's love in each of them and then among them.

In the New Testament, the word fellowship is a commercial term meaning partnership, co-operation, the sharing of trusted responsibility. Yet it has often been characterised by well-meaning but sloppy jocularity and amiability. As I think I said in a previous letter, Christian living is far more than being nice to people! And friendliness is not the same thing as friendship. An older Christian, a proven friend, a valuable fellowship – each of these has always been a *sine qua non* for believers. But never more so than now when society enforces the belief that enduring truths are not to be endured and claims of Truth are to be disclaimed. I am *not* speaking of a holy huddle but of a fellowship, a sturdy comradeship that feels and cares and is stimulating, fortifying, questioning, alive to God and to the issues of the day, together hammering them out on the anvil of biblical truth.

History – always look backward before plunging forward! – gives us some inspiring examples of fellowship. There are 1st century believers whose lives warned future generations that among the emblems of the Christian are service, suffering and sacrifice. These are normative, not exceptional. They are to be expected. One thinks of the White Horse Inn at Cambridge in the 16th century where at different times Reformers such as Bilney, Coverdale, Tyndale, Latimer, Ridley, Cranmer and Parker met in secret to "smell the Word of God". The Wesley brothers 'Holy Club' in 18th century Oxford eventually led to the Evangelical Revival and the founding of the Methodist Church. In 18th century Cambridge, Charles Simeon's work among students, his Sunday 'Conversation Parties' and sermon classes had far-reaching results for Evangelicalism then and through the 19th century. There were The Inklings at Oxford centred around C.S. Lewis, including among others, Owen Barfield, Hugh Dyson and J.R.R. Tolkien. Their friendship stimulated their lecturing and provided a seed-bed for their influential writings.

During the Second World War, a little band of Christian students in Germany were trying to evaluate their understanding of what was happening in their country. In the University of Munich they retained their sense of responsibility: "We are Christians and we are Germans. Therefore we are responsible for Germany." With concern and bravery and in naivety – this was Nazi Germany – they published their thinking in a periodical called *The White Rose* which circulated secretly among students from other universities. But like the majority of those who gathered at the White Horse Inn who were burned at the stake, many of these students paid for their faithfulness by being beheaded. These six groups of people are not only examples of fellowship, of partnership. They illustrate also some of the qualities in friendship: all are equal; each one can benefit from the gifts of the others; a moral unity emerges that strengthens each character; they stand alongside each other through thick and thin.

Let me pursue this matter of the cost of being a disciple of Jesus Christ. All these examples – there are many more up to and including our own day – show that God puts a high value on discipleship. We won't be thrown to the lions but we may be refused promotion or even lose our jobs. We may be deserted by some of our friends or even lose our lives. The history of God's people reveals that each generation has to be prepared to a greater or lesser degree for service, suffering and sacrifice. In his second letter to Timothy, Paul tells of suffering pain and even wearing chains like a criminal and knows that he is looking into the grave. Peter in his first letter to scattered groups of believers throughout the Roman empire, among them some new Christians, has this to say to them – and to us: "Dear friends, do not be unduly alarmed at the fiery ordeals which come to test your faith as though this were some abnormal experience. You should be glad because this means that you are called to share Christ's sufferings". More than once it has occurred to me that some persecution would do us western Christians much good. And it may well happen.

Dying in 1661 in a Scottish prison for his faith, Samuel Rutherford testified that "Jesus came into my soul last night and every stone flashed like a ruby." His contemporary, the preacher John Bunyan, languished twelve years on and off in Bedford gaol during which time he began and completed *The Pilgrim's Progress from this world to that which is to come.* In Africa, David Livingstone found his way from East to West and West to East, crossing the continent three times. "I went tramping through Africa", he said, "through the companionship of Christ." It has been estimated that more Christians have been martyred in this century than in all previous centuries. Some estimates give a figure of over 100,000 believers throughout the world martyred each year. Barriers are erected and deception is practised against believers – read 2 Corinthians 11: 24–33 – and lives are taken. In Canada a few years ago, at the request of some Muslims, a Christian man was jailed for three days for distributing evangelistic booklets.

You and I Richard, along with all God's people, are engaged in a war between truth and falsehood, between good and evil and it lasts all the way to the end. You will have to cultivate self-discipline and self-denial. As in marriage, it is "for better for worse, for richer for poorer, in sickness and in health". The Cross is laid on the back of every Christian and growth in godliness and usefulness depend on our perseverance over the long haul and sometimes against the odds. Is this more than you bargained for? Of course not! When fighting in a war, we're not to complain of the wounds. A contemporary adage which I like says 'If you can't stand the heat, get out of the kitchen!' But no true believer will behave like that. It is a real help when tempted to self-pity or similar feelings to recall someone, past or present, who really battled or is battling against the odds. The poet John Milton was blind for the last twenty-two years of his life with his great work *Paradise Lost* still to come. I think of a severely disabled friend from whom I have learned much whose radiancy of Christian living is infectious.

Before the raising of the Iron Curtain in Berlin in 1989, I regularly and guardedly wrote to a Christian student in Moscow who for a time was sent to the Gulag. I recall being deeply moved when reading of another young Russian Christian, Vanya Moiseyev aged 18, who was conscripted into the Red Army. On discovering he was a Christian, officers and men tried to force him to renounce his faith. But, often literally, he stood firm night after winter night outside in summer uniform in sub-zero temperatures. Enduring pain and torture, he continued to witness to Christ and endeavoured to share the gospel with any soldier who would listen. Not understanding that he would rather die than renounce Christ, Red Army soldiers went too far and his death ensued. I find it a chilling thought to realize that 'witness' is the literal rendering of a Greek word that means 'martyr'. This fine young man exemplifies to where witnessing may lead. Look up Revelation 12:11.

Every good wish

Donald

WHY BOTHER?

Dear Richard,

Thinking back to some of my recent letters about taking a stand and sometimes having a rough ride as a follower of Jesus Christ, reminds me of a student to whom I was introduced a short time ago. She knew that I was a believer and we had a friendly conversation. Towards the end she asked me this question: "Why should I bother with all this stuff? I've had no need for it so far. I've got it all."

I often come across that answer when talking with students. This is how I answer them. Instinctively I ask the Lord for his help. They need to be taken seriously and to sense the love of Christ through my redeemed humanness. And I need to remember never to believe that an unbeliever believes in his or her unbelief. Ultimately and invariably, such beliefs about life are negative and dark.

Then I ask some of these questions: What do you mean by "all this stuff?" What *do* you believe? Do you find that satisfying intellectually and helpful personally and socially? What do you believe about the meaning and purpose of life? Or is there no meaning or purpose? Why do you think that way? Do your choices matter? Do you believe in right and wrong? Why? What are the things you love and treasure? To what do you attach the greatest importance? What would you go to the stake for? Having "got it all", are you satisfied?

In response to some of the questions, I then say that I have tried to show that both of us have a common concern for the world, for meaning to it, for hope, for facing up to the fact of death.

Most students, consciously or unconsciously, are postmodernists; they deny truth, certainty and meaning but, being human, long for some kind of meaning, some 'reality'. I try to push them to the consequences of their denials.

I finish by giving a clear, simple statement about biblical truth and saying that is also a truthful world-view. Also I point out that the Bible knows *us* and leads to a restored relationship with God through repentance and faith in Jesus.

Afterwards I thank the Lord for having been in my head and in my understanding, my heart and my thinking, my mouth and my speaking. In later conversations, I may use the following quotation from Anselm, one of the early church leaders: "I do not seek to understand so that I may believe. I believe so that I may understand. And this I also believe: unless I believe, I will not understand." For that opportunity and all the other occasions that may ensue, the only response is to be found in Ps. 115:1.

Yet such conversations seem to be rare. Among your contemporaries nowadays, as you can confirm, there is not as there used to be, much tolerance of Christianity or any other 'religious options'. Rather there is developing an anti-Christian attitude which means that Christian truth and morality are usually not on anyone's agenda. As you may have heard it said, "Christians are immoral, power-crazed or even fascist". Such language, stretched beyond breaking point in meaning, is – I say this carefully – covering chasms of ignorance, irrationality and prejudice. And I would not be surprised if such language was first heard from a lecturer or tutor and also found in some text-books. There's more to be said on this subject and I'll hope to write about it another time.

So what do you as a follower of Jesus Christ do? In no particular order, stick with staunch friends. Pray together. Search the Scriptures together. Do you and your friends have some older Christian as a mentor? Ask for home and local church prayer support. Do not be ashamed. Do not be afraid. If and when possible, engage by talking about what you know and understand. Avoid arguing. Look to the Lord to win the person or persons, not you to win an argument. Keep on saying what you believe to be true. If you can't answer some questions, frankly say so but also add that you will try to find the answers. Be friendly and courteous. Your loving and listening attitude to abuse, ridicule or accusations of ignorance is far more valuable than rabbiting on.

Re-reading this letter puts me in mind of a Headmaster I know who was chatting with one of the cadets in the Combined Cadet Force. The ironic exchange went like this:

"How's it going?"

"All right."

"Do you enjoy the CCF?"

"S'all right."

"Will you stay on next year?"

"Dunno yet."

"So what are you learning this afternoon?"

"Communications."

Best wishes

Donald

A GREAT EXAMPLE

Dear Richard

I do thank you for taking the time to write and am pleased that you would like to know more about Martyn Lloyd-Jones. He was a minister who had great influence on post Second World War students and other folk and has continued to be widely read ever since. I have chosen to write about the Doctor (as he was known) rather than a living person, for several reasons. First, a living person has not yet completed his or her life. Secondly, Lloyd-Jones was a world-wide figure, revered for his many gifts and achievements. And thirdly, his ministry and influence through books, tapes and CDs continues.

When I first met him after attending a service at his church, I had been a follower of Jesus Christ only a year and was asked, too soon, to lead the older teenagers' group at my church. Having just read his first book, *The Plight of Man and the Power of God*, I gave every one a copy intimating that studying it would be a rewarding antidote to perpetual ping-pong! I thought he might like to know his book was being used in this way and when informed of this he asked me to call on him when I was next in London. This I hesitatingly did and had the privilege and pleasure of a life-long friendship with him. I am for ever in the debt of that manly, honourable and kind man and cannot estimate how much is owed to God for such a faithful friend.

Martyn Lloyd-Jones was born in Wales in 1899, spending his early years in a happy, united family and dying in 1981. Having decided at the age of sixteen on a career in medicine, he sailed through St Bartholomew's Hospital Medical School in London and graduated with distinction in the qualifying examination and with distinction also in three higher degrees that he chose to take. A professorial post awaited him but from student days working among slum-dwellers in the East End of London or as a consultant examining the rich and powerful in Harley Street in the West End, he came face-to-face with three things: the fact of sin; the fact that nominal religion had nothing to say to any patient; the question whether or not he himself was a Christian.

A number of influences led to his becoming a follower of Jesus Christ. Soon after that, believing that some doctors spend too much time enabling too many of their patients to return to some of their former sins, he decided that, noble career as it is, Medicine was not for him. Turning his back on fame and fortune, he eventually became a Congregational Church Minister and for thirty years ministered at Westminster Chapel in London. He preached three times a week to congregations numbering seven or eight hundred people and was a prince of preachers. A sermon usually lasted fifty or more minutes and he knew that God's way to the heart is through the mind. He despised pulpit techniques and manipulation but could be fiery. His preaching regularly had echoes of the Socratic style and invariably took the form of a reasoned argument: biblical, doctrinal, evangelistic. It was always 'logic on fire'.

But Lloyd-Jones was also a pastor's pastor, reaching out warmly and supportively to ministerial colleagues of all ages and denominations, helping them gain and regain confidence and significance in their calling. All his rich gifts were dedicated to the glory of God: academic medical achievements; phenomenal mind and far-ranging intellectual and literary pursuits; a unique preaching gift; beautiful family life; writing and advising; unswerving pastoral commitment and concern for people.

What is his legacy? I mention only a few bequests: the injection of a revived biblical scholarship and confidence into British Evangelicalism; a resurgence of trust and confidence in the Scriptures and their gospel proclamation; an insistence that Evangelicalism is neither a synonym for fundamentalism nor a tributary of orthodox Christianity but the river itself which has flowed from its biblical source through 2,000 years; encouragement to the Christian student world by speaking and advising; assisting in laying the foundation of IFES (International

Fellowship of Evangelical Students) and helping to establish the first evangelical biblical research centre, Tyndale House in Cambridge, as well as the London Bible College and the Evangelical Library in London. Of all these endeavours, if you were to ask me which is the most far-reaching I would say the power of biblical preaching: a church is challenged, Christians are fortified, unbelievers are converted. There is much more that I could say, but hope that this brief account of a life surrendered to God through Christ may challenge you and some of your contemporaries because Truth and its truths have to be fought for not every now and again but in *each* generation. If you would like to know more about him, please let me know and I will suggest a biography.

Never more so than today do we need heroes, not celebrities or personalities, but heroes, people who exhibit greatness of soul and noble achievements. Each of us needs heroes and Martyn Lloyd-Jones is one of mine.

"Whose faith follow."

All good wishes.

Donald

PS. In the second paragraph, I have used the phrase ' a follower of Jesus Christ'. To that phrase could be added: 'in union and in communion with him,' by which is meant that a true believer in Jesus is, as it were, joined to Christ and enjoying his companionship. When asked what I think or believe, I use this phrase rather than saying ,'I am a Christian' (although in letters, I may use the latter to make a variation). This phrase serves two purposes: it deflects attention from the unlikely possibility of the usefulness of a casual discussion about Christianity and more important, reflects attention on to the person of Jesus Christ. And it has to be *Jesus* Christ, for today Christ is considered to be one among several world spiritual leaders, like Buddha or

Mohammed. 'Jesus the saviour from sin' at once identifies him as unique. John 12: 26 defines what is meant by being such a follower: "If anyone would serve me, he must continue to follow me; to cleave steadfastly to me, conform wholly to my example in living and if need be, in dying. Wherever I am, there will my servant be also. If anyone serves me, the Father will honour him." The writer Os Guinness captures the thrust of these words as meaning that "disciples are not so much those who follow as those who *must* follow".

My comment about emphasising Jesus applies also when one reads of the recurring and pointless polls about the existence of God. Today, the word 'God' can mean anything anyone wants it to. But Jesus Christ is the issue.

PSS. Thanks for phoning, would you please ring me once you are comfortably settled into the holidays!

A GREAT RESOURCE

Dear Richard,

Thank you for your phone call asking for some Lloyd-Jones' book titles. Here's one within the range of your pocket and a good one: *Martyn Lloyd-Jones: A Family Portrait,* by Christopher Catherwood, published by Kingsway. One can also purchase CD's of many of his sermons.You also mentioned that I have several times spoken about L'Abri but not said enough to give you a clear idea of what it is. I will try to do that now; no more snap-shots but a proper photograph.

It would take too long to tell why and how Francis and Edith Schaeffer and their four children found themselves in Switzerland. L'Abri Fellowship (French for *The Shelter*) was "founded" in 1955 when one weekend they opened their home in the mountain village of Huémoz to the Swiss student friends of two of their daughters who were students at the nearby University of Lausanne. On the strength of one of the daughter's assurances to a fellow-student, "My father will answer your questions", L'Abri unknowingly began. More and more students came who wanted honest answers to honest questions about the age-old issues of 'life, God and the universe'. The Schaeffers perceived God's hand to be in all that was happening and believed that provision of food and shelter, staff and other necessities would follow calling, and be a demonstration that God really is there. Their uniqueness was not in exercising God's gift of faith or even in the significance they attached to prayer. It was in their setting out to demonstrate that there is a God who is there and that he is real, one evidence of his reality being continuously answered prayer.

L'Abri's 'philosophy' is simple and based on the belief that Christianity is true because the Bible is true. 'Christianity is not a religion or a religious option. It is the truth about the way things actually are and from that explosive fact emerge two important issues. The first is that the Bible can openly be discussed rather than blindly accepted. It can be taken seriously and considered intellectually and honestly. Secondly, because Christianity is true, it is true in every area of life. It provides a world-view encompassing all intellectual, artistic and practical endeavours. An honest Christian mind saturated in the Scriptures and well read can be brought to bear on all areas of human life.'

These two significant issues bring into focus the fact that the God of the Bible exists and the evidence is not only through rationality but through the *reality* of seeing prayer answered and lives changed.

L'Abri in each of its seven branches is a permanent home to several families who open up their homes to students who are usually between 18 and 30 years old, although older people are equally welcomed. Each day, apart from one day off each week, students for half a day help with maintenance, cooking or gardening which are necessary to keep the community functioning. Such activities are also an opportunity to put into practice the lessons learned in serving one another. The other half of the day is allotted to study, the programme of which is regularly discussed with one's tutor and may also include any personal matters. There is no fixed curriculum; students use the cassette library of over 1,800 tapes, augmented by nearly 50 L'Abri books and other volumes. A central place for teaching and learning are the meal-time discussions. There are also regular lectures.

True to its founding principles, L'Abri has never asked for staff (originally referred to as Workers), for financial support, for students or for anything. Instead, it has prayed and continues to pray for these and other needs and for people. An example of the latter is praying for the Lord to bring 'the people of his choice at the time of his choice'. This prayer too has always been answered so L'Abri although full, has, even in the early days, rarely been impossibly over-crowded. The God who is there graciously and faithfully demonstrates that he is still there.

Each of the branches in Switzerland, Holland, Sweden, United States (two branches), South Korea and England (begun in 1971), exist according to the principles which I've mentioned. When I was working in the Swiss branch during the 70s and again in the 80s, hundreds of young men and women and older folk, many in the 70s *en route* to India to sit at the feet of a guru; a few dodging the draft for Vietnam; others opposed to the war there; some escaping from what they regarded as impossible homes or fundamentalist straight-jackets; still others perplexed by existential philosophy and emerging Eastern mysticism converged on the village of Huémoz, in the early days to the understandable surprise and sometimes annoyance of the villagers. A large number of those who "came to mock, stayed to pray" while others left, often to return.

I recollect one such, Bob, a long blond-haired young rebel from Harvard University who had left the U.S. because he perceived no foundation for the actions that students in the protest movement were taking and was disillusioned because they were providing no answers. He did not wish to be involved unless he had an answer. Like many students and others who arrived at L'Abri, he had heard in youth hostels and railways stations that there was a so-called 'hippy commune' in a mountain village where for ten days one was given free meals and a bed. He was lodged in the châlet where I lived and as for a number of others, L'Abri was his staging-post for roaming round Europe. This young man was an intellectual to his finger-tips and could argue the hind leg off a donkey, denying that there was any such person as God or any such thing as truth.

But although impressed by L'Abri's critique of contemporary issues – which he accepted – and the staff and others living consistently by their beliefs – which he admired – he could not accept the basis of biblical truth as the answer. Like a number of people, he accepted the critique but not the solution. After a few days he left. Francis Schaeffer's words weighed with him: "Don't hurry but hurry up. There really are answers to your questions. But hurry up. Respond when God's reaching out to you." He soon returned and a few nights later, about two o'clock in the morning of 19 May 1970, I felt myself being shaken and heard his voice urging me to wake up. I knew what he was about to tell me: "Donald, I've become a Christian". A daily Bible study in Paul's *Letter to the Romans* began a few hours later!

There is a postscript to this story. In Sweden, one of his friends, Diane, heard of his return to L'Abri and hastened to rescue him from the clutches of what she perceived to be a cult only to find herself, an equally brilliant and lovable person, compelled to acknowledge and submit to the claims of God through Christ. They later married and the subsequent Christian influence of these two and their family cannot be estimated.

A similar story may be told of another young hippy , Roger, who rode into L'Abri on a motor-bike with a girl-friend on the pillion. In every way equally engaging, intelligent and argumentative, he fought God's truth like a terrier with a rat. While at L'Abri, he became a Christian. There, he too met a splendid, lovely girl, Marcia, and like the other family, each of them and their children are living as God would have his people live. These two accounts are only samples of several thousand men and women who came to L'Abri confused or rebellious, who were thoroughly converted. They are now doing their duty to God and their fellow men and women by daily trying to live out the truth through pushing back the darkness and letting in the light. Believing prayer was and is answered and lives were, and continue to be, changed.

As I sense, at least in the West, the encircling gloom of evil, scepticism, despair and signs of desperation, I recall reading of an incident that occurred in 1780 at Hartford, Connecticut, U.S.A. At noon, the skies suddenly turned from blue to grey and by mid-afternoon to a deep, ominous black. It was, if not a Christian, certainly a religious age and believing that the Day of Judgment had arrived, many fell on their knees and begged a final blessing before the end came. The Connecticut House of Representatives was in session and a clamour arose for an immediate adjournment. Colonel Davenport, the Speaker of the House and a man of strong faith, got to his feet and silenced them with these words: "The

Day of Judgment is either approaching or it is not. If it is, I choose to be found doing my duty. I wish therefore that candles be brought." L'Abri, a little candle of a work, by God's grace continues to shine and do its duty.

I hope you have a clearer idea of what L'Abri is. I look back with thankfulness upon the years spent there as one of the most deepening and far–reaching experiences of my life.

I am now going to pause and have my afternoon tea, sipping from what the poet William Cowper referred to as "cups that cheer but not inebriate". In fact, I shall drink a toast to Spring, for snowdrops and crocuses are yet again peeping through the soil!

Best wishes

Donald

CHRISTIAN BOOKS AND BOOKSHOPS

Dear Richard

I frequently wonder how your studies are progressing! That they are not regressing, I have no doubt. I hope you are steadily nibbling or occasionally devouring what you can already see is important and consequential. Hard work is necessary but what is just as important is *steady* work. Establish a disciplined routine and stick to it. The other day I dipped into a book on mid-Victorian education and was amused to read of E.W. Benson, then Headmaster of Wellington College, who was incapable of wasting time. Every day he walked and always with a book to read. While shaving, he read the Greek Testament! Speaking of this prompts me to say something about Christian books and bookshops.

I expect we both agree that it is better to have Christian bookshops than to have no Christian bookshops. But how much better it would have been if Christians had requested their local and other bookshops to stock Christian books. Bookshops by their nature are inclusive. Christian bookshops are exclusive. Had Christians been permitted, some say, in the selection of books in a local bookshop, those shops might still have a significant number of Christian books. With the exception of university and similar large bookshops, most local bookshops stock only New Age or contemporary cultish books. The title 'Theology' has virtually vanished and been replaced by the catch-all 'Religion' or the nebulous 'Inspirational'. Specifically Christian books may be being squeezed out in a way similar to omitting a subject from a university course of study and thinking that nothing is being taught because of that omission.

The educationalist Sir Walter Moberley observed, "It is a fallacy to suppose that by omitting a subject, you teach nothing about it. On the contrary, you teach that it is to be omitted and that therefore it is a subject of secondary importance." A similar thing is happening to Christian books in local and some other bookshops.

I think, and I say this carefully, some books – all well-intentioned – should be squeezed out, those, for example, that are what I call 'how to' books and the glut of often superficial super-spiritual books which are – again I say this carefully – often mush for the toothless. Serious Christian books should neither be diverting nor entertaining as such, nor make readers feel good about themselves. The image culture claims to do all these things for us, with minimum disturbance of our minds! Books by their very nature should enable us to grapple with ideas. The writer Dorothy Sayers remarked that the "average Christian is about as equipped to do battle with a convinced Marxist as a man with a pea-shooter is facing a fanfare of machine guns." Sadly, we are no longer primarily a nation of book lovers and book readers. But books, good books nourish minds and spirits as good food nourishes bodies.

The books I think that Christians ought to be buying and thinking about are those that illuminate the great doctrines, themes and issues of the Bible reinforced by the richness of biographies and autobiographies. Books of this kind are like mining for coal and finding seams of gold. Apologetics – *apologia* and *kategoria* – books defending the faith and books going on the offensive, should find a place and certainly those books applying Christian truth to contemporary issues. Nor would I want to forget those describing missionary endeavours and the occasional sensible and enjoyable novel. We need to read books that are both appetising and nourishing, books that we can get our teeth into. John Wesley warned his preachers that they could never be deep preachers "without extensive reading any more than a thorough Christian."

It is not generally realized that in Britain too many Christian publishers are publishing too many books to a saturated clientele. What I would like to see are not only new titles but reprints of old classics, some of which are becoming available. As usual, and I quote him again, C.S. Lewis hits the nail on the head: "We need the books that will correct the mistaken attitudes .... of our own time and that means old books .... provided they are true .... they contain those truths of which our own age is neglectful." So all things considered, I think it is better to have Christian bookshops than to have no Christian bookshops.

However, would that only books were sold! I say this gently but in my opinion some of these shops are discredited by selling tinselly trinkets and *kitsch*. The intention behind such items is, I hope, worthy: to fortify believers in their Christian living and to encourage those seeking for the truth. Others would say the intention is crassly commercial. But the result, on the whole, I am in no doubt, is one more way of marginalizing Christianity and of excluding 'outsiders'. This is not to deprecate the dedication of those willing volunteers who sacrificially work in a number of such shops. But, I believe that the sort of things I've mentioned simply reinforce the secular world's view that, as has been said, Christianity is the bearded lady sitting in her tent at the edge of the fairground.

I'm going out to lunch with a surgeon friend of mine with whom I used to climb at Zermatt in Switzerland. When ascending the Wellenkuppe, we lost our way and found ourselves slipping and sliding on shifting shale, a dangerous situation in which to be. Eventually we got on to the ridge, shaken but thankful to the Lord. What memories!

Best wishes

Donald

WHY BOTHER WITH LITERATURE?

Dear Richard

This bee in my bonnet buzzing about books needs to be exorcised! Never mind the alliteration; how's that for a mixed metaphor? Your phone call the other evening telling me you were "getting stuck into" Hardy's *The Mayor of Casterbridge* warms my heart and prompts the writing of this particular letter. As you've found, there's only one way to start and that is to go for it. In his tale *The Golden Key*, the writer George MacDonald's heroine encounters the Old Man of the Earth: "Then the Old Man of the Earth stooped over the floor of the cave, raised a huge stone from it and left it leaning. It disclosed a great hole that went plumb-down. "That is the way", he said. "But there are no stairs!" "You must throw yourself in. There is no other way." Go for it!

Think backwards. Do you remember when you first fell under the spell of a book? In what way did the magic work? To what did it lead you? Try to answer those questions because the answers should help to move you forward in developing an appreciation for literature. Why not discuss what you're reading with friends? I read recently of a church minister who, when someone comes to him with a question, pulls a book from a shelf and tells his visitor to read this or that. Only then will he discuss the problem. What is he doing? Not only is initial help being offered but that person is also being made to think about and become attracted to books. With me, the magic began with my mother reading to us from Johann Wyss' *The Swiss Family Robinson*, my identifying with the characters and being swept up into their lives. It has been like that ever since and I earnestly hope it will be the same for you and that some of these thoughts will cheer you on as you adventure into the "realms of gold".

Great literature and other artistic achievements present a panoramic sweep of all aspects of human life in such ways that we may understand their purposes and possibilities more fully. One writer, Ernest Raymond, put that this way, "Literature makes us not only feel more things but feel more about them." Horizons of thought are widened, sympathy is deepened and experience is vicariously enlarged. Vivification, a heightening of imagination and perception, is aroused and acquired.

The creative gift of imagination aids us in forming a mental picture of what is not actually present to our senses. In so doing, we can enter with sympathy into the profusion of human emotions by being initiated into those emotions and experiences through the moral splendour of, for example, Homer's *Iliad* or Tolstoy's *War and Peace*. In so doing, as C.S. Lewis observed, "I become a thousand men yet remaining myself." The great books are also trumpets of transcendence announcing for those who have ears to hear, that humanity does not inhabit a universe without purpose or meaning. In the vivid sentence of David Wells, a theologian friend of mine, "There are footprints in our world whose size and shape speak of Another." Moreover, Truth and what is morally right are not divorced.

Today, this conjunction has virtually vanished but that is not so with the great books. Please don't take these remarks to imply that most of contemporary literature is suspect, morally lethal and subversive! That is not so for there are contemporary novelists and poets whose work may be read with both pleasure and profit and followers of Christ should be among the first to say so. Despite the perpetual thrust of visual images and in some quarters, suspicion of the written word, contemporary literature flourishes. Certainly – and I say this carefully – the pseud and the phoney are still being manufactured in a number of university English Lit. Crit. factories. There is a school of thought that asserts that the meaning of a book can never really be known so we create our own meanings. Christians, of course, disagree. Did not God disclose truth through the written word?

Great literature levers us out of shrivelled feelings and narrow thinking, offering fresh nourishment and new understandings. Also – are you not finding this with Hardy? – in 'the Classics' are to be found a depth and breadth of language from the magisterial to the felicitous that may bring tears or send a shiver down the spine. Words, "when exquisitely arranged" can suggest " wonderful and indefinable sensations and impressions." This is a further reason for reading the great books. I feel privileged to be able to read and speak the English language. The poet Walter de la Mare's lines come to mind: "The sea washes England / Where all men speak / A language as rich / As ancient Greek."

Great and good literature defines true reality and testifies to enduring truths. And though there is no agreed definition of great literature, as has been said there are three requirements for it: aesthetic, didactic and moral qualities of a high order, for example, Sophocles' *Electra*, Shakespeare's *Hamlet*, Milton's *Paradise Lost*. Such books exemplify greatness, genius, uniqueness. Equally important, they completely transcend race, class and gender.

Because it is essential, I have left it until last and that is this: to evaluate and critique a book is not the first thing to do. It is never the first thing to do. But there is a time to do it, a time critically and carefully to examine what we read. Great and good books like drama, painting and music, artefacts and the natural world require from us nothing less than submission, bending the knee. We should think thoughtfully about what we're reading. But we are not to sit *on* literature but to sit *under* it in the attitude of a disciple, a learner. As we read, we slowly experience a sense of wonder. Certain words in a certain order create thoughts and emotion and lead to wonder, wonder at *what* has been said, *how* it has been said and *why* it has affected me. Humility before enduring truths, accumulated wisdom and the proper weight of History are always rewarding.

Also rewarding is the delight of spending unhurried time in an antiquarian or good second-hand bookshop. One is surrounded by 'carefully crafted silent witnesses' to great writers and scholars of the past. These witnesses are clothed with "stitched, hand-made paper, with hand-tooled coloured or gold-tooled leather binding the edges of their pages dusted with gold-leaf." For me –

and I do hope it will be the same for you, Richard – there is a sense of awe in the feel and smell of such books.

All good wishes and I hope you are encouraged in your reading. If I remember rightly, it was the writer Henry Zylstra who said that "there is more of you after reading Thomas Hardy to be Christian with than there was before you read him. There is also more conviction that you want to be". If I may say so, does that not point towards your reading another Hardy?

I recollect a VI former in one of my Advanced Level English classes who at the end of his last term said to me, "Sir, I don't think you've taught me much but you've given me a passion for poetry." I was relieved to hear that I hadn't completely failed him!

I hope *your* studies are going well!

All good wishes

Donald

SOME QUESTIONS TO BE
ASKED OF LECTURERS

Dear Richard,

The other day I was listening on the radio to a scientific discussion and was again reminded of the pursuit in Britain of the many different divisions of science and the existence of the influential scientific community. There is the equally powerful influence of the media. And I wondered what lectures you might have this week, and that question lies behind this letter which I fear may be as long as some others have been! Although we've discussed it, let me recall the background of contemporary academic thought.

Some years ago a speaker in his Commencement Address at the University of Harvard deplored the *zeitgeist*, the spirit of the times, when he remarked, "We have been taught that we can believe anything we like – as long as we do not believe it to be true". Is not that a fearful, heart-rending statement? Of course there are pockets of resistance to such foolishness but in general that is actually true. The topsy-turvy state of academia is succinctly exposed by noting the suppositions – that are invariably elevated to propositions – which support many academics in the Western world in their thinking, teaching and writing. These are then absorbed by their students. Here they are: "There are no objective criteria for determining the truth of a fact or the worth of an idea. Values and moral categories are projections only of biological or social norms. History is irrelevant. Literature consists of meaningless symbols. All study is constantly open to questioning and to reinterpretation, regardless of other considerations. Approximation is a sign of the genuine scholar while accuracy is that of a hide-bound pedant. No proposition is so certain that its opposite may be excluded. No aims are worthier of pursuit than any other aims."

These are not the meanderings of some poor soul in a lunatic asylum. They leave me reeling and should you! Let me add a postscript to that. In some universities and colleges, the quest for knowledge is prostituted by what have been called Minnie Mouse courses in, for example, "travel and leisure", "feminist theology" and "lesbian cultural theory" where, in the last two, political slogans masquerade as academic enquiry. One day, perhaps, a 'university' will appoint a Professor of Speculative Learning! Have you encountered one or more of these eight assumptions? For you, it might prompt another pertinent question: in view of these suppositions and beliefs, what am I doing here?

There's no doubt that the seed of these and subsequent ideas was sown during the 18th century Enlightenment. It was then that statements of fact and statements of value (or morality) began to be divorced and this, as those suppositions declare, is common practice today. For hundreds of years, scholars and intellectuals would rightly have regarded such suppositions as evidence of alarming and profound intellectual and moral confusion and arrogance. I imagine that the majority of students now either find nothing abnormal in these ideas and, or, feel they are in no position to challenge them. But, ideas have consequences.

There is another matter that should be realized which is that universities exert not only a powerful influence on students, but the scientific establishment which proceeds from and remains within universities exerts an absolute authority over many crucial areas of the nation's life. In Dr Johnson's great *Dictionary*, the first definition of 'Science' is simply 'knowledge'. That definition has spawned a conglomerate of specialisms dominating much of the nation's life. It is our universities which lay claim to define what constitutes knowledge. That monopoly largely interprets *what* society thinks and also *how* it thinks. The main point is this: in the Western world, the fundamental assumption concerning all knowledge is Naturalism expressed as Postmodernism. We've talked about this.

It is a fact that whatever the academic scientific community endorses becomes normative. It is also a fact that the octopus–like organism known as the media has tentacles that stretch and reach into every aspect of each person's life in every part of the western world. And of course that includes the Internet, which, like the media, can have a positive purpose. But its negative effects lie concealed: there are no checks or quality controls. What's more, the computer does not necessarily provide knowledge. It gives vast amounts of information. Knowledge has to do with the perception of fact or truth, their implications and extensions and leads to understanding. As you use your computer, Richard, make sure you're not crushed under its chariot wheels!

Don't worry; I'm about to come to your rôle! You can see from where this unchallenged position originated: Darwinism, as popularly understood, mixed with Marx's social analysis plus the addition of Freud's psychoanalysis. And there are more recent sources. In the minds of the academic establishment of the Western world, this cocktail worked like yeast (please forgive another mixed metaphor), while from the beginning of the 20th century and gaining momentum, scientific Naturalism has reigned supreme over higher and lower education.

Non-scientific subjects are assumed to have derived from or are attached to scientific ideas because as the writer Philip Johnson pointed out, "Once science has provided knowledge ..... various subjective ideologies can fit their belief systems into the framework of knowledge thus provided." For example, Christianity may be taught but it has to be taught as one of the world's religions. It is not true as the sciences are true. Therefore it is not knowledge. Religion and morality are presumed to be products of natural selection and of the chemistry of the brain. It seems that today, we are in the position where only what scientists approve is considered to be knowledge.

Many lecturers now, as the writer Steven Garber has said, "gather data, finish and publish experiments or compound interpretations but on the whole do not promulgate anything that could be described as wisdom". On the face of it, this is pretty grim. But you and your friends can help yourselves and can make a difference. Why shouldn't *you* be the mouse that roared?! Ask your lecturers questions. Bring your critical, sinewy mind to bear on what you learn and read. Refuse to become a sounding board for others' opinions. Of course lecturers and writers know more than you do. But that does not mean that what they know or all they know is true. They are not gods and you are not sheep. The presuppositions in lectures, the hidden agenda in books – you really need to uncover them. Discuss lectures, books and essays among your friends.

Courteously request a lecturer to clarify some point while you keep on probing until you understand. Then if necessary challenge. And on occasion, several of you at the same time should challenge him or her. You are not pieces of putty to be squeezed into a certain shape! After a lecture, why not with some friends invite him or her to a pub lunch to discuss some issue? In any event, ought we not to be praying that sceptical academics should be saved? You could pray for one or two known to you. We believers should certainly be asking God to help Christian academics to stand firm and bring a credible biblical perspective to bear on current secular theories.

We've talked about this and discussed some of these questions which I'll repeat here. In your subject, make sure you receive honest answers to such honest questions as: 'In advocating new theories to be accepted or positions to be adopted, are they legitimate? What are the tests? In these ideas, is reductionism at work? What revisionist ideas need investigation? What is being repudiated? Is reality being redefined? "A new age needs new scientific approaches" – perhaps, but who said so? When and where was it said? What was meant and what is implied? What are the likely consequences for believers and unbelievers? What views of human beings and of humanness are being raised? What does Scripture have to say concerning these issues?' And as for great or good books that are asserted by your lecturers to be out of date, C.S. Lewis would urge you to ask some uncomfortable questions: 'Why has it gone out of date? Why is it said to be discredited? Was it ever refuted and if so, by whom, where and how conclusively? Did it merely die away, as fashions do? If the latter, that tells us nothing about its truth or falsehood.'

Suspect innovation. Question the merely novel. Challenge. You want and you need the truth so think through some – you'll never manage all – of those questions, selecting those appropriate for your purpose, and speak up. Don't necessarily do this on your own. As I've suggested, take a lecturer out to a pub lunch but with your friends, and courteously make your voices heard. It should make a difference to him or her, in what way neither you nor I can say. Do not remain silent, Richard! Look up Nehemiah 2:4. The circumstances are similar.

Very briefly, from where are many lecturers and text-books deriving their ideas and theories? If there is such a oneness as truth today, it is conditioned by the prevailing culture. It is not God-given, authoritative. It then follows that anything claiming to be truth is allowed. I imagine that you and your friends have been urged to use this 'post-modern methodology' in your studies. If that is so, then in seminars and essays you will also be expected to conform.

A further dangerous extension of this way of thinking is that it can become automatic in all situations and relationships. No truth means that I'm left only with my feelings as a guide. I can't fall back even on conscience because I can no longer know whether conscience is telling me the truth. And as there is no truth, it's what I feel that counts. postmodernist (or rather post-Christian) thinking, if one gives it a foothold, puts society (and that means you and me) in the position where no person or authority can affirm that something is right and something else is wrong. To this stage in their destiny since the Fall, have many human beings arrived. May I suggest that we talk about this further when we meet? In the meantime, on no account copy the father who said to his son, "It is better to sit still and listen and let people think you are stupid, than to open your mouth and remove all doubt."!

In a book I was reading the other day, I came across one of Martin Buber's *Tales of the Hasidim* which bears on the thoughts in this letter. "When Mendal was already the far-famed and much-hated rabbi of Kotzak, he once returned to the little town in which he was born. There he visited the teacher who taught him his alphabet when he was a child and read the five books of Moses with him. But he did not go to see the teacher who had given him further instruction and at a chance meeting this man asked his former pupil whether he had any cause to be ashamed of him. Mendal replied, 'You taught me things that can be refuted for according to one interpretation they can mean this, according to another, that. But my first teacher taught me true teachings which cannot be refuted and they have remained with me as such. That is why I owe him special reverence'."

I earnestly hope you have found or will find such a teacher.

All good wishes

Donald

SOME QUESTIONS TO BE ASKED OF FILMS, BOOKS AND TELEVISION

Dear Richard

Your further kind phone call encourages me to make hay while the sun shines and add a few more useful questioning tips. You are not studying English, I know, but you'll get much more out of a book or a poem if you ask some of the following questions. These are of value too after having seen a play or a film. Most folk entering a cinema leave their critical faculties at the box office so when the film is over their invariable comments, if positive, are contained in a monosyllabic adjective such as 'wow, great, good, brilliant, cool.' I'm not getting at you or your peers, you know that. What I'm saying is that although ephemeral, a film cannot but affect one's state of mind and emotions. Moreover, much creativity has gone into the making of the film and therefore it deserves considered evaluation. Yet numbers of today's films – there are exceptions – are on a scale of toxicity unknown in the history of cinema. This should cause no surprise.

Having just written these words, I must eat humble pie for I'm reminded of a friend and myself in the early 70s seeing Fellini's *Satyricon* in Geneva on our day off from L'Abri. The entire film was salacious and orgiastic yet its presentation was an artistic triumph. To borrow an analogy from the Art world, the painting stank of rancid sex, the frame was a work of art. We were both bowled over, left the cinema actually groping for the staircase bannisters and slightly staggering, found a coffee-house where we talked and talked about what we'd seen and by so doing brought to the surface the visual images that had sunk into the sub-conscious. Verbalising acts as a surrogate and necessary emetic. As film and TV film makers know, the immediacy of the visual at the time can be more powerful than the verbal and it is essential for viewers to evaluate thoughts and feelings. If critiquing is not an active part of entertainment, then one becomes a passive subscriber to the untruthful or immoral suppositions, often post-modernistic, of much media presentation. One may also become subliminally affected oneself. Guilt by association is no less guilt.

Even though it's one-sided, a letter is said to be the next best thing to a conversation. And Dr Johnson may be right in saying that "questioning is *not* the mode of conversation among gentlemen". But I do not think he is! Nevertheless, here are some suggested questions. Because of technical advances and the 'immediacy' and realism of many contemporary films as well as the fact that material is screened that even five years ago might have been censored or forbidden, we should recognise that much of today's film experience overwhelms thought but raises emotion to a higher plane than before.

Here are some questions, and some of these I may have read elsewhere:: what kind of person do I think made this film/wrote this book? When was it made/written? Has the director/writer been affected by contemporary directors/writers? If so, how? Has the director/writer accepted, developed or rejected the cinematic/literary conventions of the day or created new ones? What connections are there between this work and other art forms of the time? What are the director's/ writer's presuppositions? What questions are raised? What answers are given? What comprehension of truth is revealed? What truths emerge? What view of history is presented? What view of man and woman is held? What is the director's/writer's criteria of humanness? What view of relationships is advocated? Has the director/writer performed any moral or intellectual somersaults? To what extent can you identify with the characters? If not wholly, at what point and why do you withdraw? What does this film/book *mean*? In what direction is the overall thrust? Is it well filmed/written? Is it well that it should have been filmed/written at all? And two after-thoughts: 'How does one account for Hollywood's flouting of Christian convictions by playing about with religious themes? I know *Titanic* is now film history but what is one to think about an industry which can exploit the fact of dreadful suffering caused by an actual appalling tragedy and run a parallel and utterly improbable story of two star-cross'd lovers?'

If you want to, you can skip the first six questions but the remainder should lead to a deepening of thought and feeling and give you and the friends with whom you could discuss them some satisfaction, adding another room to the building of your thought-life. The whole process will give you more confidence when talking with non-Christian friends. Of a film, you might say you agreed that the story was composed of realistic situations and real characters but that the director's conclusions were morally bankrupt. Time and time again, viewers are exposed to evil and desensitising portrayals which may leave some unbelievers either unmoved or barely stirred.

The believer may similarly be affected but is, one hopes, also made alert to what is happening within him or her: 'what I'm seeing and hearing is blasphemous and immoral and I must stand against these lies.' And when the film's over, ask the Lord to help you speak with a holy boldness and a gentle spirit. You can hold your own in argument and are endowed with an intellect that I consider is alert, acquisitive and critical for which I am sure that you are thankful to God. When the opportunity is right, use it carefully to tell your friends the truth. One result of this will be that you will have grown in moral and spiritual stature.

This morning, I saw my first goldfinch and green woodpecker of the year who came separately to have their breakfast. As usual, plump pigeons looking like Jumbo Jets landed and took off. Since living in this pleasant, quiet cul-de-sac backing on to a wood and fields, for which and the suitability of my home, I daily thank the Lord, I have had twenty-seven different species of chirping, chirruping, cheeping and croaking birds in the garden and enjoy them all, especially the despised cheeky one our Medieval forefathers called 'Philip Sparrow'! I know next to nothing about ornithology but I love watching and hearing them.

Every good wish

Donald

FORGETTING TO REMEMBER:
RECONSIDERING HISTORY

Dear Richard,

Many happy returns of the day! I hope this letter and a card reach you to wish you another worthwhile and fulfilled new year.

I am glad that you are cheered by realizing that we believers are the successors and heirs of those who through the centuries have, as Paul put it in his letter to Timothy, "fought a good fight, finished the course, kept the faith". On your birthday, this is an appropriate time to remember. Church history, or as I prefer to call it, Christian history, is nowadays largely neglected, even discounted in some quarters. Yet, to my delight (and I hope yours) History and archaeology programmes fascinate.

The contemporary philosophy of postmodernism has abandoned absolutes and certainties and relativized them. Thus Truth has deteriorated into something that becomes a matter of opinion: you have your truth, I have mine; right and wrong do not enter the discussion. I know you meet this daily among your contemporaries even though people cannot live this way.

Why has this happened? We've touched on this before, as you know. There are several reasons but here are two. Injurious aspects of Greek and Renaissance thinking have come full circle: despite misgivings and contradictions, "man is the measure of all things". Secondly, the God-given unity of knowledge has been overthrown. That process took a step forward in the 17th century when Louis Moreri produced an encyclopaedia arranged in alphabetical order. Until then, encyclopaedias were arranged according to the animal kingdom, plant kingdom, celestial kingdom. In the 18th century, another Frenchman, Denis Diderot published his *Encyclopaedia* which also had the entries arranged in alphabetical order. Because of Enlightenment thinking, this was considered especially significant. Nothing had its fixed place anymore.

History, in certain academic circles, is then up for grabs. At best, it is minimised, at worst, it is irrelevant. By accepting the premises of relativism and some of – and I say this carefully – the more imbecilic extravagancies of political correctness, new schools of History have dumped the past with its intellectual traditions and cultural artefacts. It is perceived by many people as an incubus that impedes 'progress', itself undefined and uncertain. postmodernism, driven by technology, thrusts us into the future which dislocates us further from the past. We dare not be thought to be in a time-warp.

The effect of relativizing History is, as the American historian Gertrude Himmelfarb says, "to mute the drama of history, to void it of moral content, to mitigate evil and belittle greatness". Forgetting to remember deprives us, individually and nationally, of land-marks and of signposts. We lose a sense of direction and may even change our destination. It has been well said that "nations write their autobiographies in three volumes: the book of their deeds, the book of their words and the book of their art. None of them can be understood without reading the other two". It may be argued that a human being is no more significant than an animal unless he or she is viewed as part of the warp and woof of an ancestral tapestry we call History.

Throughout Western Europe, there is a state of amnesia concerning the past. 'For generations, History has been understood as a reasoned and reasonable record of the past, especially of human affairs. It focused on constitutional, political, social and intellectual matters and was written as narrative. Its view of Progress was guarded.' Writing History on the grand scale and no doubt aware of their own presuppositions, were men like Gibbon, Macaulay, G.G. Coulton and G.M. Trevelyan who were respectful but not uncritical of the past and of the documentary records of the past. These and other historians fully understood that, as has been said, "to be ignorant of what happened before one was born is to remain a child for the whole of one's life." One's understanding of and respect for the present are in some way inhibited. Winston

Churchill is correct: "To test the present, you must appeal to History".

I can hear you saying, "This is not a letter; this is another lecture!" So be it! You know this subject is one of my chief concerns and one of the reasons for the falling away of some Christian students, in that they do not realise that the truth they believe in and live by has an historical beginning and continuity to the end of time. Without this awareness, people can feel intimidated, uncertain, begin to doubt and wander. The writer G.K. Chesterton correctly stated both cause and effect: "Any man who is cut off from the past.... is a man most unjustly disinherited". The German poet Goethe was even more emphatic: "He who cannot call upon the last 3,000 years has to live from hand to mouth." This permissible exaggeration makes the same point as Chesterton who, I believe, would have asserted the God of the Bible as initiator and lord of History, the one who promotes, permits and will terminate History. I look forward to our meeting again some time when I guess this subject too might be on your agenda!

When you phoned, I forgot to thank you for asking about the moles in my garden. The transformation of a new lawn into a fairground switch-back by tiny archaeologists demolished my *Wind in the Willows* perception of moles! But now I've made up my mind to live with the evidence of their digs only because deterrents don't appear to deter and because I could not bear to have them – or is it, it? – to be poisoned or trapped. I am trying to feel honoured that they have chosen *my* garden! A molestation of moles makes the writer Charles Frasier's depiction of the mole as "a little powerless hermit blind thing propelled by lonesomeness and resentment to bring the world falling around him", endearingly disturbing.

Best wishes

Donald

FORGETTING TO REMEMBER:
THE LOSS OF A CHRISTIAN MEMORY

Dear Richard,

As one gets older, one of the minor irritations are the daily lapses into forgetfulness, what the Americans delightfully refer to as "senior moments"! I mean coming into my study for something I remember I need yet having no idea why I'm there; alternatively, coming into my study and leaving with something for which I *didn't* come. Life for me would undoubtedly be easier if only I could remember that I forget!

These minor irritations bear, of course, no comparison whatsoever with the grave consequences that have afflicted God's people through the running centuries when they have forgotten to remember. Throughout the entire scriptures, God himself and his messengers, particularly Moses and Joshua in the Old Testament and Jesus himself and Paul in the New, repeatedly urged believers to remember, recall, recollect, remind themselves, in effect, of who they are and whom they serve. The entire scriptures from time to time recapitulate the disastrous consequences of forgetting to remember. Today's believers are in that same position. We suffer from amnesia. In recent years, an almost total eclipse of the significance of Christian history has taken place. You may ask why this has happened. There are a number of reasons. I will be brief!

First is the theory of reductionism, that a fact or idea is 'nothing but' such and such or 'no more than' such and such. Secondly is repudiation which asserts that all cultures are equal, all values are relative. Thirdly is revisionism – this is a legitimate pursuit, the other two are not – which calls the past into question for further investigation. Fourthly, post-modernism believes that the past inhibits both present and future. As I have said before, we must ever appear to want to break with the past. Fifthly, recent church initiatives like the mega-church movement in the U.S., the 'prosperity' or 'wealth and health' gospel and some high-profile revivalism have a tank-like impetus and a clamorous drive that surge irresistibly onward. Sixthly, confronted in the 60s by the permissive society and some legislation that has helped to change the course of our moral history, many Christians lost their nerve and retreated into a church area of activity.

You may ask: taken together, what are the consequences for believers of ignoring or even riding roughshod over the past? Think about it. First, when our backs are turned on History, we deprive ourselves of the light that illuminated earlier Christians' problems and ours. We are unaware of heresies that had to be defeated, some of which are with us still. Secondly, to ignore History means that we are bereft of heroes and heroines and have to make do with – I say this gently – a lesser breed altogether: 'celebrities' and 'personalities' famous only for being famous. "It is great events" and great people, not only famous people but great little people, "that define the life and memory" of a nation. And thirdly, without a grasp of History, our steps as a nation will inevitably be hesitant and pragmatic. We cannot study the future. But we have studied the past and that gives us a perspective on what to think and in which direction to go.

Edmund Burke's warning is dire (in its original meaning): "They will not look forward to their posterity who never look back to their ancestry." An illustration of this neglect of History is to be found – and I say this gently, and not nostalgically – in some worship services in the usurping of older hymns by contemporary songs. By no means are all older hymns well written or set to princely music. Yet their endurance is an indication of their quality. My concern is that students and congregations generally, are unwittingly being dispossessed of their historical, cultural, literary and poetic heritage. It is a fact that the Wesley brothers replaced some old hymns with their own. But the reason is not far to seek: they considered that many hymns sung in the Church of England insufficiently emphasised biblical doctrines.

I hope I have shown how important it is to know at least the outline of our Christian legacy. To the Jews, 'to know' meant not only to be in possession of knowledge or information. It imposed also a responsibility for dealing with that knowledge. I hope also that before too long you will find time to acquaint yourself with Christian history which covers the time from the first apostles to the present day.

Let me mention three readable, succinct and short books on the subject. The first is *The Story of the Church* by A.M. Renwick and A.M. Harman; the second is *Valiant in Fight* by B.F.C Atkinson, a scholar and friend from university days; a third is one concerned specifically with the Reformation: *The Reformation* by Kirsten Birkett. These valuable books will add to your library although Atkinson's book may be out of print. If you become more interested in Christian history, you couldn't do better than invest, volume by volume, in the *Penguin History of the Church* and, as with all reading, keep your wits about you.

I'm off to bed. Napoleon used to eschew a good night's sleep and settle for brief naps of say, ten to fifteen minutes. Winston Churchill observed a similar pattern. But I need, or think I need, unbroken hours of sleep wrapped in cosiness! I'm ready to rise at 6am all year round. Then comes my time of listening to God followed by a large bowl of "guid Scottish porridge". My father was half a Scot and maybe that has something to do with my life-long love affair with it!

Every good wish and sleep well.

Donald

PS. A friendly little note from your sister tells me she has her university place for next year. I am pleased for her.

CHRISTIANITY IS UNIVERSAL TRUTH

Dear Richard

Thank you for ringing and thanks to the Lord for his faithfulness to you. Look up Psalm 40: 1–31. I do hope your sister is settling into her nursing well and I know she realizes that nursing is about giving, as well as emptying bed-pans or the modern equivalent!

Here is another letter to my young friend, a follower of Jesus Christ who is privileged to live in company with fellow-followers who have nailed their colours to the mast of truth or, if you prefer, to the Cross of the risen Christ. Perhaps that sounds highfalutin, a little grandiose, but it's a fact and it does us no harm again and again to remind ourselves aloud of this and humbly to thank God we are united to the truth as it is in Jesus. Also from time to time we are challenged by non-believers and expected to have a credible reason for believing. In one or two past letters, I've touched on this but am moved to return to it now, knowing that your CU is preparing for a mini-mission soon to take place. Do please keep me informed. I hope these few crumbs will provide a small snack!

I'm not about to produce a carefully argued apologetic or verification of Christianity's claim to be the truth. There are more qualified people than myself to help you do that. But here are some preliminary, elementary thoughts when one is seeking a world-view that alone claims to be the only Truth and to make sense of life and reality.

From the Enlightenment onwards, we have been mesmerised by the assumption that modern science and philosophy have permanently destroyed the intellectual validity of the Christian faith. In addition, Eastern religions and a mushroom-like sprouting of other world-views including Paganism, now claim equality. But for any claim to veracity and credibility, there must first be a basis in reality. In an earlier letter, you will remember I discussed this. John Wesley's model of the Christian faith was that of a quadrilateral of truth comprising scripture, faith, reason and experience. The claim of biblical Christianity is that it is true and offers sufficient evidence to say that it is, in Francis Schaeffer's phrase, 'true Truth'. Moreover, as theologians Lesslie Newbigin and Francis Schaeffer before him argued, it is not only private truth. It is universal truth and speaks not only to the 'religious' part of life but being the truth about human life and destiny, addresses each aspect of human activity.

It does this because it is true to the reality that actually *is*. You may remember that I discussed this in a previous letter and on the phone. The Bible presents the need for each individual to be right with God and his provision for that through Christ's death and resurrection. But that is only one part of the gospel, the good news. The other part is that the Bible frames a world-view. As an individual who is created in God's image but fallen, sinful, I need redeeming, being brought back by being bought back. It is the same with the universe. It was created good. It fell. God provided for its redemption. Christianity is the only world-view that tells the truth about creation, the fall and redemption. God created the stage. We perform the play through scenes that declare human beings' mandate from God to set the world to work domestically, agriculturally, industrially, artistically and scientifically. Would any of these propositions be accepted by a postmodernist?

Newbiggin argued that the Bible is "a narrative that structures human experience and understanding. However varied be its texture, it is essentially a story that claims to be *the* story, the true story both of the cosmos and of human life within the cosmos". And if there is a story there must be a story-teller. It is universal truth in that its message is for all peoples. It is universal truth also in that it is concerned with the *polis*, the people and where they live, its institutions and its community. But this universal truth is frequently privatised under the impact of today's secularism and scepticism. Instead of being glad – not foolishly proud but inwardly reassured when we think and act differently from unbelievers – we often feel disoriented and then diminished. Through the centuries, true believers have felt this but have rallied, not been ashamed and have stood their ground, for example Joseph and Daniel, Peter and Paul. Some of us should feel ashamed as we wriggle like a hooked fish. In an explosive sentence, Os Guinness blows apart our excuses: "The problem with Western Christians is not that they aren't where they should be but that they aren't what they should be where they are." And where is that? It is anywhere we happen to be living, witnesses to living truth.

Even though I've suggested some tentative thoughts about the foundations for establishing a true world-view, I know as you do that the majority of students are not interested in any *apologia*, defending the truth, any more than they are intrigued by *kategoria*, going on the offensive. As I have said, logical reasoning is not a feature of the post-Christian landscape. There is no more reason for believing in Christianity than in, say, Zen Buddhism or a Flat Earth or any of the more *outré* beliefs popular nowadays. In any event, who cares? Many of your contemporaries will tell you too that evangelising is unforgivable.

Students and others cling to social and cultural *mores*, traditional and experimental, and the glue that holds them together is that trampoline word, relationships. And of course such are vital, for whenever human beings find themselves thinking about 'life, God and the universe', they eventually feel a shiver of deadness, emptiness or, at least, disappointment. That trio spears specific questions such as: Is there anyone there? Is there any meaning in Truth? Is it worth even asking any questions? Such questions are cries of pain as well as the fear that, as Ecclesiastes says, all is emptiness, falsity, futility and vanity. That deadness has to be pushed away. In order to allay present anxieties and anaesthetize future fears, the self then clamours for an anodyne or for some excitement which the entire entertainment industry is ever on hand to provide.

As I have said before, the classic formulation of these eternal questions is that of Gauguin's painting. The Christian, though, has a guaranteed future. There is no time when he or she is ever separated from God through Christ. Because of your redeemed humanness, I know that you care and during the mission will be walking along and staying alongside an unbelieving friend or two, showing Christ's love, simply 'being there'. As the next Generation X slides further into the prevailing nihilism and fatalism which are already miasmic, steady faithfulness in friendship can be used by God ultimately to direct unbelievers' attention to biblical Christianity where "will you find no fair, false promises but the sharp comfort that doth spring from truth." I hope this helps a little to comfort, to strengthen you at this time.

The other day, I visited another art exhibition in London, this time of Jackson Pollock's paintings. He is the American artist remembered chiefly for his abstract drip-paintings. Famously and unfairly dubbed Jack the Dripper, for those he used industrial paints and flicked or dripped the paint on to the canvas. They look like giant webs or a high aerial photograph of London or any big city.

I do hope you will become interested in looking at great pictures. In an earlier letter I said that great art and music, literature and architecture enrich life so much. Try this for yourself! Go into a gallery. Slowly move along. A painting arrests your attention. Stop. Gaze. Do not ask any questions about it. Let it work its magic on you. There is just you and the picture, no one else, nothing else. Receive, welcome what that picture is saying to you. Stand, stare for as long as it takes you to absorb. If you wish, then ask yourself some questions or make comments.

A life-long love-affair might have begun. Today's unlovely jargon calls it 'interaction'.

Best wishes

Donald

A FURTHER BRIEF NOTE

Dear Richard

I know you're going through a difficult time just now and there are occasions when we do feel like giving up and throwing in the towel.

Do you know Winston Churchill's memorable address to the pupils of his old school, Harrow, in October 1941? This was the entire speech: *'Never give in, never give in, never, never, never, never – in nothing, great or small, large or petty – never give in except to convictions of honour and good sense.'*

Say these noble, true words aloud! Don't feel self–pitying or guilty about having a difficult time. That comes not once or twice but many times to all of us. Read aloud also the first eleven verses of Paul's second letter to the Christians at Corinth. We can only surmise why he was so distressed. Perhaps he was undergoing an 'identity crisis' or been told that he wasn't smart enough! Whatever it was, he not only pulled through but triumphed by refusing to listen to himself or to others and choosing to talk to himself before the Lord, to get up and go on.

You too, Richard, are to do the same. So am I, for I too get weary and low.

Best wishes,

Donald

PS.   There is a Dundee cake on its way to you!

THE CONSUMING CULTURE OF CONSUMERISM

Dear Richard

Recently, I drove one of my student friends back to university. Jam-packed in the car park were parents and students repeatedly diving into the back of their cars and emerging, as my friend did, with boxes of CDs, a computer, a fax machine, Hi-Fi equipment, multiple speakers, pots and pans, one or two small boxes of books, a suitcase presumably containing clothes, sports gear of different kinds and once, the comforting sight of a teddy-bear. I couldn't help recalling crossing London and boarding the train to Cambridge with two suitcases, one of books, the other of clothes! The script for this scene might have come straight from Pink Floyd's album *The Dark Side of the Moon*: "Grab that cash with both hands and make a stash."

It was an apt illustration of how consumermanic our society appears to have become. Consumerism is dealing not only with the week's shopping, in person or via the Internet. For many shoppers in the U.K., it is "Tesco+ *ergo sum*": I shop, therefore I am, or even, I shop in the hope of becoming someone else. The way we appear, the choices we reject, the choices we make, the credit-cards we flash – these can enhance our identity and self-esteem. But if the truth be told, we are slaves. The world happens to be organised on the basis of producing, buying, selling and possessing. And we are expected to adapt. Consumerism entices, promises, focuses us not primarily on needs but on wants. For each 'need', each anxiety, some product somewhere is at hand. Options and choices, not so much necessities, seem to be the overwhelming considerations within purchasing power, even though the country is "awash with Coca–Cola and stamped on by Reeboks." Subjectivism, what is true or right for *me*, operates for most people in most areas of modern life. I know of an English

---

+ For American readers, Tesco is a supermarket chain.

millionaire who has twelve luxurious cars. Shopping malls are our new cathedrals, wherein we slavishly worship.

The force that moves all us slaves around is advertising, supremely TV and newspaper advertising. There's much that could and needs to be said about TV advertising but I want to make only two comments. Bombarded by advertising, the visual and the immediate, fortified by forceful or subtle suggestion and innuendo, exert considerable subliminal sway over emotions and mind, whatever the product. It is as though consumerism was being promoted as a complete way of life. Secondly, some advertisements subtly incite to untrammelled self-expression, for example this one from Calvin Klein: "Be good, be kind, just be. Calvin Klein ' Be' perfume." The invariable result is that we get on a treadmill of spending, coveting and consuming which frequently leads into debt. Marketing regards people as materialistic objects "pulsating with appetites for more of this and more of that and those objects are to be flattered and stimulated, whether they can afford the goods or not." Marketing is no respecter of anyone or anything. Most of us are victims who go on foolishly imagining that money is always the solution whereas it often proves to be the problem. For the huge number of poor, marginalised, abused and disempowered folk – who are far more in number than we suppose – there is no solution. It's all problem, misery and pain. We should cry for them.

In the 60s, the academic Marshall McLuhan showed that there is a message in the actual fact of the existence of TV itself. From once reflecting reality, TV now seems to have the power to create it. As with cinema, its essence is deceit. The writer John Benton helpfully notes five reasons for TV winning the game: "The message is that what you see is what is true; material reality is all there is. It captures attention .... and shuts down inner reflection. The things we see cannot hurt us and blunt our moral sensitivity. It delights our eyes (for) the viewer is the most important thing. It provides a channel-changer and a multitude of options and says, 'You choose'." Now you know why I refer to my TV as Polyphemus;

he was the one-eyed monster in the poet Homer's poem *The Odyssey*. In this connection, an essential and excellent book is the academic Neil Postman's *Amusing Ourselves to Death*. Do read it.

Consumerism is a cast of mind, an attitude of acquisition, partly for acquisition's sake and partly sometimes for ostentatious reasons. The most ostentatious American consumer symbol that I can think of is the voluptuous stretch limousine, gleaming with glamour, oozing opulence, twenty feet of vulgarity and decadence. Nowadays, there is so much money available if one is able to get one's hands on it. And a consumer greedily becomes possessed by possessions and obsessed by anticipated possessions he or she doesn't yet but intends to possess, e.g. 'the breathtaking superiority of those trainers!' Consumerism via TV is paraded as the turnstile to 'the good life'.

The torrent of materialism (not the philosophy but the amassing of things) with its implacable appeal to greed and therefore likely selfishness, knows no obstacles and no boundaries. It flatteringly glides into the defences of unbeliever and believer alike with its smooth promises of happiness and shameless lying about the true purpose of life. It can turn us from being sensible and discerning customers into "fashion- conscious and impulse-driven consumers." And should we be unsure of who we are as persons – not to mention who we are before God – advertisers will assure us we are 'real' and 'someone' only when we purchase this or that. Tailor made, "it has your name on it." You may soon be able to buy your own brand or blend of cornflakes! To breed yet another *cliché*, we must consume to live but now we live to consume. Yet, as Jesus said, "What good can it do a man to gain the whole world at the price of his own soul? What can a man offer to buy back his soul, once he has lost it?"

Covetousness and greed, plus the spending of more and more money, swiftly become an addiction. Western Europe has perfected the craft of greed, and virtues like self-denial, patience and self-control do not seem to exist. Sometimes affluence accentuates arrogance. As John Benton has also pointed out, sixty years ago one's 'identity' was fixed by gender and class. Today, one can choose one's own identity or status symbol where choice is elevated to a virtue. These impediments are also dangers for the follower of Jesus Christ. Self-fulfilment is never God's purpose for any human being. Salvation, rescue is his purpose and one of its components is contentment. For the believer, the battle lines are drawn: covetousness or contentment. And by contentment, as used by Paul in I Tim. 6;6, is meant a sense of inward sufficiency and is a constituent part of godliness. But, as has been said, your generation, believers or unbelievers, are a pushover for the ad-men.

It's not wrong to have money but it is wrong for you and for me to make its acquisition and spending a prime aim. God's agenda for his people is crystal clear in I Timothy 6:6–10. We have to keep on looking to Christ day by day and especially on shopping days! Christians have to lean very hard,very hard indeed, against today's pressures, against what Scripture understands as a part of worldliness. I am convinced that the greatest *folly* of the West is ignoring God. But possibly one of the greatest *threats* to the West is self-indulgent permissiveness, the lemming-like pursuit of pleasure, which includes consumerism. And for Christians, this pursuit of Pleasure is nothing less than the sin of idolatry. Some of us have forgotten that "Jesus calls us from the worship of the vain world's golden store, from each idol that would keep us ....."

In the light of what I've been saying, is it not startling to recollect that the Bible's injunction is that it is the longing for money, the lust for it, (lust means: 'I must have it at once') not sex or fame but money, the love of it, that plunges people into acute mental pangs and sometimes ruin? In contrast to the 'good business' of godliness, it does not pay. No wonder Luther spoke of three necessary conversions: the heart, the mind, the pocket! Money is necessary. The love of money is lethal. Money is only a tool. I beg you, do not allow it to become an idol or an obsession.

I am sure you have heard of the wealthy farmer whose agro-business produced so much grain that he had to demolish existing barns and build larger ones. His pride and self-satisfaction got the better of him and he retired, throwing himself into 'the good life'. One night God spoke to him and said, 'You fool, you thoughtless man. Tonight you will be asked for your soul'. I have wondered what happens to today's driven ones. In Greek mythology, the Furies excited men to crime and then threw them into madness. Sadly, perhaps something of that is the lot of some who go the whole hog.

Jesus' story reminds one that, as the writer Mark Greene has observed, "the pressure for rising consumption has destructive consequences in terms of the increasing gap between the rich and the poor with its potential for social and political disaster, in terms of environmental sustainability and most seriously of all perhaps, in terms of its deadening effect on human moral sensibility." These accurate statements or worse, forecasts, should be in our thinking and living and provide talking points with friends and neighbours. I'm ashamed to write this, but last year to the poorest nations of the world, Britain gave a derisory 0.22 per cent of its G.N.P.

In passing, the National Lottery in Britain has contributed to a number of 'good causes'. But its enticement to cupidity is demoralizing in that it is producing a hardening greed for consumerism, not to mention much self-inflicted suffering. What then gradually results, for who knows how many people, is a sense of what the Bible speaks of as "emptiness, falsity, vainglory and futility." John Wesley's common-sense advice in one of his sermons is sound: ... "the fault does not lie in the money but in them that use it....Gain all you can, without hurting either yourself or your neighbour; save all you can, by cutting off every expense which serves only to indulge foolish desire; give all you can or, in other words, give all you have to God. Do not stint yourself...." Also, as I said in an earlier letter, establish sensible home budgeting. Practise tithing or some equivalent and carefully and as generously as you can, apportion money for people and charities of your thoughtful and prayerful choosing. And remember: Credit =Debit!

In Britain as in other wealthy countries, we accumulate so much and at the same time are daily made aware of the misery of the poor. What action should we take concerning them? And do we need all our possessions? Many of them have taken up residence in our home because, as Colson & Pearcey correctly say, "the religion of consumerism is like drinking salt water: the more you drink the thirstier you get." Whether it is comestibles, cars or take-overs, the root impulse is greed. And sooner or later, conspicuous consumption, perhaps unrealized, may be followed by conspicuous constriction.

You will soon have to think more about these things. In the meantime, remind yourself that possessions *per se* can and do clog our spiritual arteries and weaken our distinctive witness. The development of Christian character will become enfeebled and the virtues of self-denial and thrift vitiated. It seems long ago now but I remember my angry reaction to a bank's advertising its credit card as: 'It takes the waiting out of wanting'. Watch the TV advertisements if you must. But turn the sound off and ask them who they think they're kidding!

In a western world of consumerism and greed, live sensibly yet simply. Be for, and have time for, the hungry and the downtrodden. Don't only *have* faith. Put it into *practice*, Richard, otherwise you and I, are deluding ourselves.

You could have a productive discussion with your friends on this subject. Why not quote Jesus' statement from Matt. 16.26 and follow through the reaction? On this subject, what do you think is *the* question for believers?

One of the curses of consumerism is so many cars and lorries. Did you know that *every* day there are on average 20 million cars on British roads? And did you know also that *every* day there are cars with an estimated 10 million empty seats? Many of these could be filled, thus reducing the number of vehicles and the amount of pollution. Thoughtlessness and selfishness are often twins.

Best wishes

Donald

PS. Two useful little books on this subject are *Money isn't God* by John White and *How to get really rich* by Brian Rosner.

WEDLOCK OR DEADLOCK?

Dear Richard,

Thank you so much for making the effort to come over last week. Such occasions are valuable for opening wider the windows of heart and mind and I really enjoyed our time together. I was intrigued that you mentioned marriage because I would not have considered that it was a subject much thought about by students. Let me recall some of the main points about which we talked.

I heard the other day of a young man who had attended a church wedding who remarked afterwards, "It appeared so *final.*" It seemed to confirm that many of his generation continue to think that it is impossible for a genuine and full life to continue after such a public and private pledge. To my mind, the *Book of Common Prayer* has no equal in stating what are the purposes of marriage for all men and women. Christianity is universal truth and although the marriage service in some form is obligatory, special, gladsome and heartfelt for believers, it is meant for all folk. One hopes that unbelieving couples will not assume they are believers but scent its biblical truths and find Christ, and that believers will continually throw themselves on the mercy and plead the grace of God for their walk and witness together.

Nowadays, for many people, marriage is virtually 'out'. Have not the rôles of men and women, fathers and mothers, been redefined? Are not masculinity and femininity said to be artificial 'social constructs'? Therefore cannot men marry men and women marry women? The foolishness of politically correct dogma does away with distinctions, regarding them as sexist, whatever that means. Feminism, originally necessary, has sadly deteriorated into militancy, hostility and competitiveness. It has succeeded in watering down the meaning of masculinity and femininity, wearing down the natural necessity for men to become manly, gentlemanly and for women to become feminine, womanly, and demeaning motherhood.

But there are many people who do decide they want to marry in the normal way. Others will ask questions such as: 'why marry anyway? Settle for a partner.' What secular genius came up with *that* word, I wonder? 'Commitment need not be for life.' Or one can pitch oneself into today's loveless sexual mayhem which should make the begetters of the 60s' permissive society gasp at the genie they have let out of the bottle. Personal satisfaction now is paramount. The 'feel-good factor' is decisive. For many people today, the criterion is four bare legs in bed – always in bed if 'twere possible and whose bed and with whom doesn't seem to matter. Having a meal in a restaurant; having sex – it's all recreation. The writer Dorothy Sayers, whom David Porter in his delightful *The Monarch Book of Sins and Virtues* quotes, wrote that "we have reached one of those periods of spiritual depression where people go to bed because they have nothing better to do."

That was in the 30s and 40s. The change now is colossal to the extent that heterosexuality is by many folk judged to be outdated and repressive. You'll find a good number in the university who believe this and you need to have an answer for them. Marriage has halved. Divorce has trebled. The media, especially some films and TV soaps, seem hell-bent on trying to bury marriage. Celebrity romances catch the headlines but the message at present is insistent: marriage is dead, live together, practise serial monogamy, do your own thing, say 'yes' to anything, deny yourself nothing. In contrast, Christian marriage is exclusive and permanent, founded on complete commitment, mutual trust and intimacy and has to be monogamous, permanent and public: society needs to know. However, according to recent findings, fewer couples are getting married either in church or at a registry office with more children being born out of wedlock. And there are reasons to think that within the next ten years married couples may be an anachronism. Yet trends are renowned for their chameleon-like behaviour.

A follower of the Lord Jesus Christ has to give much thought and prayer as to whom, whether and when to marry. Before committing themselves to marriage, each potential couple should answer some serious questions: what does Scripture have to say about marriage? What is meant by the husband's 'headship'? Does that mean a wife's subservience? Is marriage primarily for sexual relief and pleasure? As has been said, there are other weighty questions: do I respect, trust, love him or her? Is she or he good enough to be the mother /father of my children? On waking up each morning for the next fifty years, do I want to see his or her face on the pillow? How do we regard each others' parents? There is no doubt whatsoever that after life-long dedication to God through Christ, life-long commitment to marriage is the most serious and far-reaching decision you will make.

What about the man or woman who would like to be married but seems unable to meet the right person? In such a situation I think one should avoid casual relationships with no kind of commitment at all. By casual, I mean going out with someone simply to fill up the time. That and flirting ought not to be options. I went out with several girls before meeting the one I thought would become my wife. You will find that a difference develops between girlfriends and friends who are girls. The former are closer and one girl may become very close. To begin with, one has, I think, to try to find the median between a relationship (that word again!) and a friendship. None of this is easy. In fact, it's impossible because one is just not interested in a 'relationship' or a friendship. What one or both are looking for, or are already consumed by, is love. In our fallen world, we have to strive to acquire virtues and struggle against not only vices but the second best.

In *that* situation, however, I do believe that the Christian should settle for struggling to keep a friendship going but not prolong it falsely. Don't lose your self–respect. As I saw it and still see it, the biblical way of conducting a close personal relationship, friendship in fact, is frankly to discuss it, fixing boundaries and sticking to them, responsibly commending or reproving each other and being accountable to a friend or mentor. Undergird all this with personal prayer and occasionally praying together. At present, you enjoy the company and affection of a number of friends. You are thankful for and feel at home in your church and CU. But if or when this issue should surface in the midst of your daily life, the paramount and permanent priority is to keep on handing it over to the Lord, pleading with him: "Please lead and prepare me for the girl /boy of your choice and please lead and prepare the boy/ girl of your choice for me. But if you want me to remain single for now or all my life, please give me the grace to be so." Let God be God in all things. This prayer, sincerely prayed when you feel the need for it, will take a lot of heat out of the situation.

In a previous letter, I stressed that becoming a believer implies among other things, sacrifice, service, suffering. Here one must add submission to God. The Christian soldier does not give but is given orders and finds, amazingly, that "in his service is perfect freedom." I say this humbly but I think this covers the heart of the matter and life can continue to be lived. Time and emotional energy are saved. Keep on trusting your heavenly father. Ask yourself this most searching question: as I have trusted God with the salvation of my soul for eternity, can I not trust him about marriage or singleness in this life?

This too, perhaps, is a foreign land, a place where you haven't been before and do not know the way and there's plenty of time to find that way. A great missionary, Amy Carmichael, comments that "the foreign land draws us nearer to God because he is the only one whom we know there." So go to him as the one you know. Everything else is strange. "But he is enough". This is yet another place to apply faith, a deliberate commitment on your part to the Lord when you cannot see your way.

I'm going to stop here because some students from L'Abri are coming to tea and DV, I'll continue in the next letter. But I can't resist quoting Ogden Nash's whimsical *A Word to Husbands*: "To keep your marriage brimming /With love in the loving cup,/ Whenever you're wrong, admit it; /Whenever you're right, shut up!"

A good book on the whole subject of relationships, singleness and marriage is *The Relationships Revolution* by Nigel Pollock.

All good wishes

Donald

MARRIAGE OR SINGLENESS?

Dear Richard,

Let me continue where I left off – but rather where *we* left off – but not before telling you that from a window looking on to my back garden, I saw something reddish-brown curled up on the grass. Yes, it was a fox! I looked at it through binoculars for about a quarter of an hour and then it glided away. I was fascinated by its appearance and like the novelist D.H. Lawrence observing a snake in his garden and letting it stay there, was moved by its choosing *my* garden in which to rest. Moles first and now a fox! Back to marriage. But you can put this and my previous letter away in a drawer until the matter really arises!

When two people are certain they should marry, an engagement period is more than helpful. It is essential. Matters to do with likes and dislikes; ways of doing this or that; uncovering attributes of character and temperament; strengths and weaknesses; things in common; anticipating certain things in the future; getting to know respective parents; allowing trust and love to put down deep roots – these matters and potential difficulties can be honestly revealed and explored and some decisions made affecting them rather than becoming potential flash-points in marriage itself.

When two folk are engaged, I write them a letter as follows: "I am writing to wish you happiness, fulfilment and blessing in your forthcoming marriage. In the belief that a spectator sees more of the game than the players, I am venturing to offer my small quota of affectionate advice. I. Begin with realistic expectations. 2. Keep your worthwhile goals ever in sight. 3. Generously define your rôles. 4. Say love as well as show love. Affectionate language, perhaps using endearing names coupled with affectionate actions, help to keep the wheels of marriage oiled and can prevent monotony and boredom from rusting it. 5. "Humbly confess your faults to one another." Keep on practising forgiveness, acknowledging this hasty retort, that hurtful comment. Refuse to permit petty pride a place. 6. "Never let the sun go down on your wrath." Do not allow disagreements to deteriorate into disputes. Clear them out of the way before the end of the day. 7. Remember that one chooses and goes on choosing to love. Of course feelings are involved. But when difficult or dangerous moments come, as they will, then you *choose* to love your wife, you *choose* to love your husband. 8. Regularly pray together.

The philanthropist George Müller was convinced that one of the deepest blessings of his married life was that in addition to times of private and family prayer, he and his wife Mary frequently prayed together. Moreover, thousands of times (he) told her, 'My darling, I never saw you at any time since you became my wife without my being delighted to see you.'

I conclude my letter by saying: "These are some of the concerns that, given persistent perseverance, will help to make your marriage work well. Keep on persevering so that your living may be a testimony to truth and beauty before a watching world." What *leit-motif* is dancing through that affectionate advice? It is that a good marriage begins with and is sustained by a sound friendship. The opposite of that is a marriage that flounders on fantasies. A good marriage flourishes on friendship. I was humbled to be told that some student friends regard these suggestions as important enough to have had them framed and placed over the fireplace in their sitting room.

As you know from our earlier discussion, I was engaged to be married. She was (and I can be sure she still is) a lovely girl of noble character, a follower of Jesus Christ. I loved her. But something was missing. I prayed. She prayed. The sardonic yet sensible saying, "marry in haste, repent at leisure" weighed with me. But what weighed far more and has lasted to this day, is the pain and hurt I inflicted on her, twinges of which, when memories come unbidden, afflict me even now.

There will be followers of Christ who eventually conclude that they have no inclination towards heterosexuality. They have to grapple with the desire to express their sexuality. Such folk must be assured that there is no sin nor condemnation in being homosexual or lesbian. But several passages in the Bible condemn being a practising homosexual. Indeed, both heterosexuals and homosexuals and lesbians have in their fallenness to fight against sinful expressions of sexuality. They must be assured also of the certainty of God's unconditional love for them and his intention and ability unfailingly to strengthen them to their lives' end. They need to know too where trusted and genuine assistance and loyal Christian friends can be found. More could be said about this subject but I will leave it at that.

What about singleness? Sometimes, there is a terrible aloneness or loneliness for a single person at university or in a job and at other times. This is especially so if one is the odd one out in a *ménage à trois* and I think that women may suffer more from being single than men. It is a foreign and can be a frightening land. Yet others are in a similar situation and one might seek them out, show oneself friendly and keep on talking to the Lord.

I think much nonsense has been uttered, both in the Christian and the secular world, about singleness. It may be caused because of an unhealed hurt or harm. It may exist because a husband or wife has died or because there has been a divorce. It is said to be a mask for being homosexual or lesbian. It is stated even to be a disease. It is to be a calling for some people. Celibacy may be a calling, and that word needs defining. Rather I consider it is a gift, a gift that Paul gladly received, not *a* gift of singleness but *the* gift of contentment. I too can truly say: I am content. It has not always been easy. But truly, I am content. Yet whether some time hoping to marry or having to accept being single, certainly not resigned to it but willingly accepting it, remember Richard that "in his will is our peace." "He is enough". As you sought his will in guidance before and found it faithfully given, so do so here. From time to time amid frustration and anxiety, I thankfully testify to God's refreshing me from that river of contentment. Moreover, I am deeply privileged and thankful to have many friends, among them young friends of different ages, countless nieces and adopted nieces and nephews across the world! In this guise, I am not alone and by God's great grace although living alone, I have never known the agony of loneliness. For that I am really grateful.

In all these and other matters, the greatest assurance, the greatest comfort as I continue to find, is to know that I have trusted God for my eternal salvation. That being so I repeat: cannot I trust him to see me through these issues? What is my faith worth to me in this matter? "I am not ashamed because I know whom I have believed and am positively persuaded that he is able to guard and keep that which has been entrusted to me, which I have committed to him until that day". He has given his word. We are saved for eternity. We can go on and will go on trusting him until he sends for us or comes again.

Please tell me if I've forgotten any points in our discussion. I hope I haven't sounded like a tutor in a Victorian household! Having just written the word 'tutor', reminds me that on one occasion when I asked my College Tutor, a marvellous man and a wit, a question that had to do with my History course, he replied, "My dear Drew, I do not know. Go to the Dean. He does not know. But he will tell you!"

I guess Finals can't be far away. Being a sensible chap, I imagine that already you have a revision programme under way. When revising for exams, I wrote down notes taken from notes on postcards, all of which were ready one month before Finals. Every day for that month and during exams, I would read them aloud three times a day. It worked. During the actual exams, there was not instant recall but there was swift recollection. I still have those postcards! Come to think of it, didn't I mention this to you before now? Allocate plenty of time for steady revision.

Every good wish

Donald

PS. Al Hsu wrote a book called *The Single Issue* which is very up- to-date and treats singleness as equal to marriage – its worth a read!

In the letter about consumerism, I asked what you thought was *the* question on the subject for believers. When we met, unfortunately I forgot to ask you. My answer, as has been said, would be, "What do I want from life? And what do I want others to have from life?"

The Day of Reckoning!

Dear Richard,

Reading something in the paper the other day alerted me to the fact that your exams are only a few weeks away. I can hear your respsone: 'There's no need to remind me!'

Yet the fact that this is so is less important than one's attitude to that fact. Some students – those like the one I mentioned in a previous letter who was sitting next to me in an exam, who looked at the question paper and then stalked out of the hall – will have reason to fear exams. Others may feel reasonably easy. Yet, probably no-one enjoys taking them, any more than we enjoy a medical examination, a driving test or a professional entry examination.

But like many things in life, any test is as much one of character as it is of knowledge or skill. You have plenty of the former and should have acquired all you now need to know for each exam. As in everything, keep on talking to the Lord about it and release the stickability, courage and determination which I've seen you summon up when rowing and racing on the river.

You Christian guys and girls have a splendid opportunity to witness to the reality of 'resting in the Lord', being calm and quietly confident of the Saviour's love and the help that he will continue to supply. Just as you talk aloud your postcard notes, make a point again and again not of listening to yourself, to your fears and anxieties, but of talking to yourself in the Lord's hearing, reassuring yourself of his presence and peace and thanking him that he will be there. When you know your results, thankfully accept them. They cannot be changed. Nor is God playing games with you. Your response (not reaction, for that is often hasty and emotional) is another test of character and another opportunity for strengthening your faith in God's faithfulness to you.

For has he not promised that he will see us safely through our lives from the beginning to the end? And that includes all the 'in-between'.

Affectionately,
Donald

MY STORY

Dear Richard

It's raining again and I've remembered a little ditty I heard years ago: 'The rain it raineth every day / Upon the just and unjust feller / But more upon the just / Because the unjust's pinched the just's umbrella.'

Oh well, that's life! You may remember that when you were leaving after the last time we talked, you asked me about my life. Well, here's a summary.

My younger brother and I were born in the 1920s, myself at Lincoln, into an affectionate church-going home, living first in Kent and Surrey and then Sussex. My father trained as a mechanical engineer but for most of his life was chairman of one of Britain's insurance companies. Summer holidays were spent at different seaside resorts but as we grew older, we motored – there were fewer cars, no motorways and far fewer roads – the length and breadth of England, seeing relatives and visiting many of our great cathedrals and castles.

In the process, we absorbed the beauty of landscape and seascape, extended our knowledge of history and geography and began to appreciate art, music and literature, until the Second World War put a stop to such travelling. We went to Culford, an Independent School, absorbing not only the beauty of Palladian buildings surrounded by 400 acres of parkland and a lake but receiving also what might be called an all-round classical education, for which I shall always be profoundly grateful. Unlike my brother, an all-round games player, I played rugger with enormous enthusiasm but unimaginable ineptitude! I thought also that I was a Christian and with the family was a regular church-goer. I was certainly a religious boy and on that account probably obnoxious!

In the holidays, we loved visits to London to some of its museums, exhibitions, churches, shops and theatres, enjoying tea in one of Lyons' fashionable tea shops known as Corner Houses. At home, we enjoyed outings in the car into villages and through woods and flower-filled fields and meadows. There were no supermarkets, no TV, no computers, no McDonalds, no NHS and no "teenagers" – the species is a post-War mutation! Of course, Britain was never the Garden of Eden. But there is no doubt that it was a safer, quieter and a more self-respecting country, far less tainted, much less complicated than it is now. There was an understood respect for the traditional family and for authority emanating from our Judaeo-Christian history. As the philosopher Roger Scruton has observed, something akin to gentleness was a characteristic then. Unconsciously, we regarded it all even as a civilization.

We listened to jazz and the Big Bands and went to the cinema (black and white films only) and the theatre. We called our friends' fathers 'Sir', raising our caps, later hats, to ladies we knew. During the summer holidays, sometimes we would stay for a day or two at a friend's home. I remember having tea at one such friend's home where his mother had provided rock cakes worthy of the name and a plate of paper-thin bread and butter which swiftly disappeared, eliciting the humbug exclamation, "Ah, I've just cut enough!"

Having left school nine months before the beginning of the War, because of my love for literature I had expected my career might have something to do with books and accordingly joined a London publishing house, the Epworth Press. A young man in the office was kind and helpful to me and I noticed that each lunch-time while eating our sandwiches, he read the Bible. When war broke out, among a number of government Air Raid Precautions was a requirement for every employer with more than thirty staff, nightly to supply fire-watching teams on or near roofs. One night in October 1940 while he and I were doing fire-prevention duty on the roof and expecting the usual air-raid, we talked, he with his pocket Bible open, and I began to understand what it meant really to be a Christian. That same night, he explained what the Bible means by sin, repentance and faith, leading me to place my trust in Jesus Christ. In the days that followed, he encouraged my first steps as a believer in Jesus and suggested that I went as often as possible to a Dr Martyn Lloyd-Jones' church in London.

During the War, I registered as a conscientious objector. This was done because I knew I could not kill but was open to serving wherever directed, and that was first working on a farm and then teaching in two Preparatory Schools, one in Surrey, the other in Derbyshire. In addition, I was on a nightly rota for fire-watching. I had thought that the Methodist Church was calling me into its ministry but through that time of teaching, God indicated my future career.

At the end of the War, I went to Emmanuel College at Cambridge – after five failed attempts to pass an entrance examination in Mathematics! – to read History, several years later reading English. While there, I was privileged to become President of the CICCU (Cambridge Inter-Collegiate Christian Union), the first of the university Christian Unions, founded on 9 March 1877. In those early post-war years, the CU was full of ex-servicemen and numbered 400 or so (which it still does).

After graduating, I was appointed a Housemaster at an Independent School renowned among other things for its hockey, St Lawrence College. I was there for twenty happy years and was engaged to be married but as I have said, that did not happen. During that time, nearly every summer was spent mountaineering in the Swiss Alps. What memories! On one such occasion I drove up to the mountain village of Huémoz to visit L'Abri Fellowship where a former pupil and friend, Os Guinness, was working and to my astonishment Francis Schaeffer invited me to think and pray about becoming a member of staff.

A year later in 1969, I went, spending four exhilarating and exhausting years followed in the eighties by two more, learning to love, listen to and talk with the lost, confused and sometimes angry 60s and 70s students from all parts of the world, who in those early years trekked (and still do trek) up the mountain to the little village of Huémoz. That whole exciting time included making many friends, a lecturing visit to Australia and several lecturing visits to the USA. Between two sojourns in L'Abri, nearly two pleasurable years as a Visiting Professor in English Literature were spent at Geneva College in Pennsylvania.

Returning to England, I was fortunate to be appointed a senior assistant English master at a Grammar School in Kent. Living now near the English branch of L'Abri and attending the church which grew out of it, it is a great privilege and delight to work with students and from time to time to speak to Christian Unions in the UK. It has also been a continuing pleasure many times to visit the United States and, while enjoying and staying with friends, also speak to university Christian groups and a generous sprinkling of student gatherings in different parts of the States.

On a recent visit, while queuing at the check–in at Heathrow for Washington, DC, I recalled the story of the irate man who was abusing the check–in clerk for a New York flight, and acting in a boorish manner. When he had marched off, the next person in the queue told the clerk how ashamed he felt at such behaviour, to which she replied, "Oh, don't you worry sir. I've got him sorted out. His luggage is on the way to Sydney!"

Best wishes

Donald

ALPINE MOUNTAINEERING

Dear Richard,

When we last met, I remember your prevailing upon me to tell you about the twenty years I spent each summer mountaineering in the Swiss Alps. In a letter, this is not an easy task but I'll try, not only because you asked about it but also because your studying Ecology would provide you, as it were, with another laboratory while your love of outdoor sports, especially rowing, suggests that you might take to climbing like a duck to water! Provided it is honourable and worthwhile, each person needs some passions that thrill and stretch one beyond one's grasp. I am humbled and thankful to have a number of such passions, which I mentioned recently, which have gladdened and continue to gladden and do my heart good and hope also that they have been and are a benison and a stimulus to others.

I am ashamed to say that I have not climbed in the British Isles and wish I had. The opportunity to go on holiday to Switzerland with some student friends precipitated me into mountaineering for the next twenty consecutive years. It was the arrival of the British in the mid-19th century which provided the impulse for Alpine climbing. They began sniffing round the mountains and 'discovered' mountaineering as a sport. Interest in European mountaineering accelerated with the historic and tragic first ascent of the Matterhorn in 1865.

I have always been deeply stirred by beauty in its multifarious forms, by the minute as well as the mighty. Mountains especially have been a passion. As I've said, one must have a passion as well as an interest in something worthwhile. We each need that. From my first sight of the lofty and proud Matterhorn, I was astounded by its situation, scale, proportions and symmetry, above all by its aesthetics and have been enabled to climb it three times by three different routes when its aesthetics were *not* one's primary concern! Mountains are there for everybody. They tower above us sublime and beautiful, creating a vision, presenting a challenge. Before a certain age, one is physically not strong enough to climb and I agree that 'the reasons that impel men and women to do so are more inward than outward.' The ascent of a hard route depends as much on mental and moral as on physical ruggedness. At the same time, as has been said, it is a curiously intellectual sport for you think with and through your body. Unsuspected qualities of character are uncovered and cultivated. One's needs are minimal. Daily distractions are non-existent. As the poet William Blake wrote, "Great things are done when men and mountains meet. / This is not done by jostling in the street."

I served my apprenticeship climbing in the Stubai Alps in Austria and then at Pontresina and Arolla in Switzerland before graduating to Zermatt. As the celebrated mountaineer Frank Smythe said, "Zermatt is more than a name. It is an age, a past, a tradition." But sadly it is no longer the mountain village I knew and loved. A way of life has vanished and been replaced by a way of living: tourism. As for the mountains, they seem to be more vulnerable than the citizens; I am thinking of rubbish discarded thoughtlessly or selfishly. Above what is now a small town rises a mighty horseshoe of towering 12-15 ,000 ft peaks and at the centre of the horseshoe stands the Matterhorn, lonely and aloof, 'like a great tongue of flame leaping into the sky.'

After settling in, one spends three days of training in order to adjust to altitudes, to increase stamina and to make muscles and joints flexible. Then my guide or climbing friends and I, would laboriously trudge the three or more hours up to the mountain hut. Leaving the town, we walk through flower-studded meadows and pinewoods and then scramble up boulders and scree to the sound of ever-running water. Here the going is steep, leading across a glacier to the hut. We meet other climbers plodding their way up to the sound of jingling pitons and crampons like ourselves, festooned with ropes and rucksacks. Inside the solid stone hut are a kitchen, messroom and dormitories with a resident warden for the season.

Outside, the darkness is deepening and the silvery twinkling of diamantine stars is appearing, "little chips of frozen fire in the dark velvet of the jewelled scarf of the Milky Way which spans the sky like a triumphal arch of misty light." And because of the height, the vault of heaven is free from pollution. So silent is it, I can hear it. So cold is it, I hasten inside to be greeted by snatches of subdued conversation in different languages and sudden bursts of laughter, while seeping through the apparent nonchalance is an undercurrent of tension and strain. It is now 7:30 pm: and time to turn in. By 3am or 4 am, the hut may be empty. A sour taste in the mouth, the stomach queasy, muscles like lead, a hurried forcing of indigestible food down an unwilling throat at half-past three on an icy morning are the prelude to a climb that may last seven or twelve or more hours climbing from hut to summit through thinning air 3 or 4,000 feet of snow and rock and ice and chimney and face and arrête and couloir and ledge and gully and gendarme.

Sleepy and taciturn, roped together and with ice-axe, crampons and a rucksack containing various necessities, we pick our way, perhaps with a lamp, across the snowfield or down the ribbed glaciers and by yawning crevasses to the base of the ridge or face that we hope to climb. My body automatically goes through the movements necessary to gain height but neither mind nor spirit is awake 'while one's heart is shrouded in dullness and doubt.' But before long, the glory of a mountain sunrise begins to be sensed and soon the sun begins to rise with a splendour like trumpets, pale pink spreading across the sky as long, low, level lines of lambent light mix with colours and shapes that do not merely merge but blend and then burst suddenly into a "pinpoint of blinding whiteness" that orbits into fullness.

One climbs early in the day to avoid as much soft snow as possible and to allow for emergencies. It is difficult to maintain balance and a steady rhythm as one claws one's way upwards. But after a few rests and some sugar lumps, the summit is reached, grateful thanks given to the guide and greetings passed to any other climbers. One then looks at the view. At the *view*? It is rather to admire from the depths of one's being the limitless panorama of snow and rock and steep and shape. It is to try to absorb as much as possible of the glory of "the land of far distances" that ranges through 360 degrees. On my first ascent of the Matterhorn we reached the summit but then the weather abruptly changed. The temperature rapidly dropped. Anvil-shaped clouds were boiling across the sky, the wind shrieking, cutting like a scythe, lightning flashing and thunder crackling. Rock that had been dry was glistening with ice, snow like globes of ice-cream pummelling one's body. I was frightened yet stimulated. It was terrifying but majestic!

I must soon finish this, otherwise a letter will become a brochure! Follow with me in imagination to the summit of Monte Rosa. The day is calm and clear, sky sapphire, atmosphere still. Gaze at the vast amphitheatre of giant peaks. None of the Alpine summits is hidden. To the west is that mighty monarch, Mont Blanc. 9,000 feet below us are the meadows of Zermatt. There is every combination that beauty can give. One crowded hour of wonder is yours when you see spread before you north, south, east and west the anatomy of those mountain-after-mountain ranges!

Stiff and weary yet reluctantly, we descend. When climbing up, one faces the mountain in order to see where to place hands and feet. When climbing down, however, one faces outward into space also in order to see where to place one's feet. Achievement is a heady tonic and combined with crushing fatigue requires vigilant care to prevent a mishap. After two hours or so we are on the snowfield that is now sodden as wet rice under which may be small holes or huge caverns. Caution is required. Eventually, we are at the hut. Like the summit, in its own way it is a great moment.

Why did I become a mountaineer? The majestic splendour of the mountains acted like a magnet. Then, like any sport, it became a love, a love for climbing. I was not concerned to "knock the bastard off" or expect the summit would always be reached but to co-ordinate limbs, head and heart and work with the structure of the mountain with respect, calculated risk, and determination, absorbed by the beauty of the mountains. Now, climbing seems to be more competitive and from time to time commercially driven, yet I am astonished and admire some of the feats achieved by today's climbers.

What do I cherish? Principally, memories, then the mountain itself and the climb itself; the reliable companionship of friends; the steadfastness and skill of guides; the silence and solitude; long, harsh days of endurance, of adventure into beauty, not only the massive but the sparkle of joy at the sight of a marmot or chamois, a soaring chough or some rock-crystals and the shy loveliness of flowers; stinging blizzards and rocks slimy as seaweed; "those little cats' paws of fear that die away again as the menacing terror is pushed back step by step and grip by grip"; the heavy hours before dawn and the daily miracle of the coming of light. And all this achieved with the minimum of equipment and fuss. And through it all, my spirit unfailingly rose in adoration and gratitude to the Creator who "in his strength setteth fast the mountains and is girded about with power". I have often said that I could and would not have climbed were it not for the assurance of the grace of God.

There is much more I could have written. Do you want to put yourself through this? I think you do. I hope you will. As has been said, mountains take your breath away! I heard of a student who on arrival at a mountain's summit exclaimed, "Wow! God made all this for *me*?" That's the spirit!

Best wishes

Donald

PS. In a mountain climb, how many parallels do you imagine there are to the Christian life? Quite a number!

THE DRAG AND DELIGHT OF DAILY LABOUR

Dear Richard

"The letter written, the friend's forgot. I'd friends remember so I answer not." This cynical recipe for a quiet life is an amusing sophistry but hardly conducive to winning let alone retaining friends! Were I not a follower of Jesus Christ, I might be attracted by its last admonition but being one, I regard the letters I write not as an exacting duty but trusting they have a helpful purpose. In any event, we've discussed or touched on a number of the topics about which I'm writing.

The number and variety of careers that have long existed and many others that have been called into existence, are almost hypnotic! The wondering led to pondering about careers these days and I venture some comments that I hope may be useful. On a whim, I looked up the origin of 'career' and it derives from the Roman *carraria* meaning 'a road', hence a course, progress. You are already progressing along a road that is likely to merge into a fast motorway. You are not proceeding along it by accident but by God's appointment which you will increasingly realize as you move forward.

People in some careers today may to some extent be able to choose their conditions of work. But the majority find themselves in a business or other commercial pressure-cooker where some of these things are routine: stress is normal, long hours are demanded, difficult colleagues may be expected, absenteeism is frequent, redundancy is anticipated, certain dishonest or ruthless practices occur, uncongenial or conscience-pricking work occasionally is experienced, commuting is loathed, the cooker may burst or you may be fired. Extraordinary demands nowadays are made on performance, targets and objectives. Yet not all businesses are known as high-flying, or high lying, where honesty seldom pays and some CVs are known to have been re-written. And you may wonder whatever has happened to all that leisure that we were promised a decade ago! No longer is any career certain until you are put out to grass. You may have to search for new fields. All these exigencies are normative in a fallen world.

By and large, the workplace has been dehumanized. People and nature have been and are being exploited. Maybe what the 18th century Industrial and Agrarian Revolutions began is coming full circle. Yet for every follower of Jesus, in union and in communion with him, God has that person in the hollow of his hand. You have been sent by the Lord, wherever you are, to be a witness to the changing power Jesus brings to lives, to be part of his plan in others' lives. All the time, especially when you try to apply truth to the moral dilemmas you encounter, you will need courage and that closeness with God and the fellowship, the comradeship I mentioned in a previous letter.

Yes, your career may be lost. But not your calling as a son of the living God. Os Guinness has written a superb book on this subject entitled *The Call*. Some time read it – in small doses. God has work for you to do that no-one else should do and given you gifts in order to do it. There's always cause for thankfulness. If paid work is difficult to obtain then you may have to consider some voluntary work, perhaps an opportunity as a Christian citizen to accept some civic responsibility. Some of the knowledge and experience of your profession may be valuable and usable in a new setting. Come to terms with the fact that employment or unemployment is part of your calling. The preacher, Graham Heaps, reminds us from Romans 8 that unemployment is part of suffering which is endemic because of the Fall. But through that suffering, you will always remain a son of God. You will not be the only one. He has provided infinite resources. Any trouble will fit into his plan for your good. God is alongside you.

Many of your contemporaries will beaver away only for the money. Working *only* for money is working only for oneself. Fulfilment is only in the cheque. Of course money is important. Recently, a friend was preaching on this subject and he had, as preachers often have, three parts to the sermon: Where do we get it? Where do we keep it? What happens to it? He pointed out a sometimes overlooked fact: God is the ultimate giver to the believer for he has said that "the silver is *mine* and the gold is *mine*." We are reluctant to grasp this fact and let it grip us to the point where we are able sincerely to acknowledge that the prime reason for earning money is to be in a position *to give it away*. Yes, for the Christian, that is so! We cling to the Roman belief that ownership is outright. We choose not to remember the Hebrew belief that everything comes from God. We are stewards and there will be a reckoning. Certainly to save is prudent whereas to hoard is miserly.

As I have said, income is of course important but a Christian's aim should be that of service, service to colleagues, service to his or her employer, service to the community. To regard one's daily labour this way is not easy. The Fall changed the intrinsic nature of work but did not repudiate its daily necessity. Did you know that both Greeks and Romans regarded manual work as degrading for only slaves worked with their hands, while in Medieval times, only 'sacred' work was considered worthy? From this latter attitude stems the sacred-secular divide. The writer Matthew Henry comments that "he shall sweat but his toil shall make his rest the more welcome whence he returns to the earth as to his bed. He shall grieve but he shall not starve." The Puritans properly considered all work as part of a believer's calling. When we work conscientiously, we are "co-workers with God" assisting in pushing back some effects of the Fall. The Victorians exalted work as a virtue. Today, many regard work as a necessary evil and are bribed by big money.

But there is something honourable to be found in one's work, as the poet George Herbert knew: "He who sweeps a room as for Thy laws, makes that and th' action fine." There should be not only a duty but a dignity, a creativity to be found in daily labour. I do not think any of us has a right to work but we do have obligations within it. The way I do my work, however soul-jarring it may appear to be; the nature of the association I have with my colleagues; my understanding and application of integrity and loyalty – these are the things that secretly always count as admirable. In other words, work becomes truly fulfilling only when it is built on spiritual and moral foundations.

For many folk, attitudes to work, assisted by stress and uncertainty, can produce an inimical and unhappy atmosphere and the Christian can make a real difference there. One can demonstrate that work is not a necessary evil. How can it be when it was part of God's original creation design? Like each part of living, it should declare something of the fact and glory of God. Did not Jesus' apprenticeship to carpentry and Peter's job as a fisherman evince this?

By the same token, so should a worthy ambition. It is still true that the higher the pulpit, as it were, the wider the influence. Such things are noticed by colleagues. Do you know the story of the two frogs that jumped into a pail of milk? One despaired of survival and sank to the bottom. The other swam round and round and was soon sitting on a large pat of butter. That's ambition for you! When your time comes, look for opportunities in your profession where you can effectively make a difference in attitudes, in atmosphere. Seek out others of like mind and loyalty, take your complete calling seriously and lay solid foundations for the generation that will follow you.

In their book which I have already mentioned, Colson & Pearcey recall Solzhenitsyn's novel *One day in the life of Ivan Denisovich*, which describes life in the Gulag. Shukhov, one of the prisoners, refuses to let his true humanness die. Despite the guards' brutality, starvation rations and agonising labour, he takes pride in building a wall. "It was straight. His hands had skill in them yet." Work, paid or unpaid, is still a two-fold gift of God: beneficial service and personal achievement.

There is a 'feel in the air' announcing Summer is ready, waiting in the wings!

All good wishes.

Donald

PS. Has your father found a job yet? Please let me know.

PS. Here are some useful websites for recent graduates:
1. Christiansatwork.org.uk
2. uccf.org.uk/graduates
3. graduateimpact.com

WHAT NEXT?

Dear Richard,

Fortunately, you have obtained a good degree and have the probability of an interesting job awaiting you. But many – and it is many – graduates and others, when they were in their twenties, believed that after graduation or other attainments, they would have an enjoyable, financially secure job and somewhere pleasant to live. But for them, such situations have not materialized and they are experiencing unanticipated difficulty in making adjustments. They find they are what has been described as 'twenty-something teenagers'.

There is the fact that the work they would wish to do , for which university has helped to prepare them, is limited. The many apparent number of choices open to them has shrunk and they may become disillusioned and depressed. Some students may have few people to help them face these 'unexpectednesses'. Parents should be in the frontline for this but that is not a certainty today. Some of your Christian and non-Christian friends may be in this unemployed position.

You can get alongside them by urging them on no account to give up their hope, their dream. It is not true that 'any dream will do' but we know when we've found our dream. They must persist in remaining resolute and passionate about the work they really want to do and never lose sight of their worthwhile objective. Carefully go on repeating this.

In the meantime, encourage them to consider becoming craftsmen and women such as carpenters, plumbers, electricians as well as nurses, teachers, engineers, police and social services personnel.

You can cheer your Christian friends by reminding them to remind themselves of God's faithful, immense promises. He will never let us go, He will never let us down and you and your friends should remember and go on repeating – aloud!– God's enduring truths.

Affectionately,
Donald

ANTICIPATING THE FUTURE

Dear Richard

As I write this letter, the poet J.G. Whittier's lines come to mind: "I know not what the future hath / Of marvel or surprise...." and as I look back through the arches of the years, the truth of those words has been confirmed again and again and in every aspect of life. In your life so far, you too can say the same. And we should be profoundly grateful to our heavenly father that the future is shielded from us. Like a mountaineer, it is one step at a time, second by second into the distance.

Yet we can speculate because each aspect of life is part of a continuum. As Bilbo, you remember, says in Tolkien's *The Fellowship of the Ring*, you "will see a world that I shall never know", at least in Western Europe: an increasingly ageing population; the loss of biodiversity; global warming; a revolution in biotechnology and communications and much else. Truth as a concept and in practice may virtually have vanished. In human thinking, it is not fixed like the North Star. Behaviour, which is always hitched to belief, will inevitably become more relative because there will continue to be no fixed right and wrong.

Thus society at best will be morally indifferent, at worst, morally irredeemable, at risk because of debased individual and public behaviour. Speaking very generally, I think that the churches will become more accommodating to multi-culturalism with, in some churches, the minimising of more biblical truths. In some circumstances, like 1st century Christians, believers may find it necessary to live together and, like Eastern European believers under Communism, establish 'underground' churches. Unless Christ returns or there is a huge turning to God and he grants repentance, I envisage some or much of the above happening for you will be living in an even more alien land surrounded by heathen culture. On the other hand, our prayer should be that God may move our nation first to repentance and then to reformation and revival.

So where may all this leave you and your Christian brothers and sisters?

I'd like to suggest we might meet again to discuss this, if you wish, but know that is not possible now near the end not only of a term but of your time at university. Knuckling down to Finals and then clearing up and cleaning up has to be done! So may I make some comments and again, you might like to consider these with your friends.

In a nutshell, remind yourself of your standing, your status before the God who is there. By his undeserved favour, you and I have been rescued from sin and its consequences to love and serve him in company with others, in order to bring glory to God and truth and life into people's lives.

Secondly, remember to examine God's outliving life in you and all other issues by the infallible and sufficient searchlight of the Scriptures.

And thirdly, recollect that Christ is not only your true Saviour but the one who gives meaning and purpose to Christianity's claim to being the only true world-view.

Keep going on fighting the good fight. Keep going on to finish the race. Keep firmly holding the faith to your dying day. "*Never give in...*" And remember that in a fast–moving society, men and women of Christian conviction and principles cannot afford to fight battles thinking aloud. As Martyn Lloyd-Jones said, quoting from the Apostle Paul, "'Set your affection on things that are above, not on things that are on the earth.' You have to set them as if you are setting a compass. And you have to do this deliberately. The world will not help you but rather hinder you." In different ways, people have their God-given humanness demeaned, undermined by our prevailing culture. In a world where all truth-claims are denigrated as power-play in disguise, a strong thing that can assist in neutralising that is genuine friendliness, friendship, love. These break down suspicion and scepticism. Loving others is the way for them to be drawn to God in Christ.

I'm nearly at the end! but want to add a few brief thoughts for you. One: hold fast to your committed, affectionate and accountable friends. As Shakespeare said, 'Those friends thou hast and their adoption tried, grapple them to thy heart with hoops of steel.' Two: never let the past put a brake on the present. Three: when unsure about anything, stand on the things of which you are sure. Four: never lose your sense of wonder in simple, beautiful things. Five: be a risk-taker, not foolishly, but thoughtfully. Six: do not be afraid of failure; get up and go on. Seven: uncover your character and creative gifts and use them. Eight: Martin Luther's prayer: 'Let no man take from me the vision that God willeth to do a great work through me.'

In the film *October Sky*, a true story set in the late fifties in a small West Virginian coal-mining town, four teenagers known as "The Rocket Boys" experiment in making rockets. Homer Hickham, the leader, is fascinated by rocketry and is determined to build one. After a number of alarming and hilarious launches, town and school derision, opposition, humiliation and family disruption, a rocket is successfully launched and disappears high into the sky. Their success was achieved because they persisted with unremitting determination in believing in the reality of what they were doing and were encouraged by a woman teacher who believed in them. All of them moved into useful careers, Homer Hickham becoming a leading scientist at Cape Canaveral.

All good wishes

Donald

PS. I do hope you have bought a copy of Honeysett's *Meltdown* because it clearly deals with postmodernism, how to understand and tackle it.

ON LEAVING UNIVERSITY

Dear Richard,

So you begin your Finals next Monday. They will be a marker on the last stage, stamping a seal on three unique years the like of which you will not have again. Yet you will carry into the future a few firm and valued friendships, more understanding about yourself and other people and the acquisition not only of knowledge you didn't have when you began but of ways of acquiring, dealing with and extending that knowledge. What's more, now you can think of yourself as an Ecologist! You know that I shall be thinking of and praying for you during the exams and anxious to know the results.

Like Matriculation, Graduation Day, which is another milestone, will be the occasion for congratulations and celebrations! You will stand as generations before you have stood. Years of history will be celebrated in that event. As has been said, its graduation traditions are not to be slighted as mere frumpery performed by marionettes dressed in funny clothes. Those traditions point to a rootedness both of continuity and unity to a belief in the value of respecting and learning from the past, and to a thankfulness for the privilege of being part of that heritage.

What's more, Graduation Day not only signals the end of three or four years of university but announces the beginning of a new stage. This further rite of passage is a significant step forward for you and your friends and contemporaries. That step is one more on an adventure, on an exciting although risky venture into unknown territory. And you are ever accompanied, companioned by your Saviour who knows the territory well, in whose life you are hidden, whose grace, provided you are trusting and obeying, will fulfil your life and continue to use you in others' lives. As you grow older, thankfully and calmly ensure that in all things he is Lord of the Years.

I wonder where you'll be working in, say, ten year's time? Your noble concern for the health and safety of the environment may be dented a little by the necessity to put bread on the table. As far as possible, pursue your ecological studies for you will find that the already kindled sparks will become flames.

Never lose your vision, your sense of calling, of hope. Keep these bright for they will help to make the rough places plain and are a precious part of your integrity. Dream your dreams too. If we have no dreams, it's because we're dead. It is said that one can live 40 days without food, seven days without water, three minutes without air. But we cannot live one second without hope. I don't mean expectation which implies some certainty, nor optimism which implies some distance from reality. In the Bible, hope implies belief in what is attainable. It implies trust and reliance and is rooted in reality. The believer's hope is built on the bedrock certainty that our faith is in the God of hope, not resting on human expectations or aspirations. God promises that it is a hope that will "not make us ashamed".

It was the writer Henry Drummond who wrote that "I am part of all that I have met." As far as people are concerned, that is so. Your parents and friends and I are part of your life. You are part of mine. We are bound together in the same bundle of life. For this, I am honoured and grateful.

It has been noted that, following the collapse of Communism in 1989, an extraordinary thing occurred. Russian churches were filled with worshippers who yet had no understanding of faith. But in every family there had been a grandmother, a *babushka* who, while parents were working or attending party meetings, was teaching the children about God and prayer. She had kept the flag flying for the next generation. This too is your responsibility.

Richard, you know how much I appreciate and believe in you. Among your gifts you have undoubted leadership qualities and my charge, my commission for you is to be found in I Timothy 6: 11–16. If I can help you in any way at any time about anything, you know you have only to ask. God willing, I shall continue to keep in touch with you. Please again remember me warmly to your parents and sister.

Keep the flag flying until you fall at his feet with it!

Affectionately,

Donald

BOOKS MENTIONED IN
ORDER OF THE LETTERS

O.R.Barclay, *Evangelicalism in Britain 1935–1995*, IVP: Leicester, 1997 (A first-hand account of some momentous years of British evangelicalism).

Steven Garber, *The Fabric of Faithfulness*, Downers Grove: IVP, 1996. (Weaving together belief and behaviour during the university years).

Harry Blamires, *The Post-Christian Mind* London: SPCK, 1999 (An exposure of the way the media is trashing Christian principles in every area of life).

James W. Sire, *The Universe Next Door*, IVP Downers Grove, Illinois, USA 1997 (A clear guide book to world views).

Marcus Honeysett, *Meltdown*, Leicester: IVP (An easily read analysis of postmodernism; essential reading).

C. Colson & N. Pearcey *How Now Shall We Live?* Tydnale, 1999 (Showing that the great spiritual battle today is a cosmic struggle between competing world-views – The title is not to be confused with Francis Schaeffer's *How Should We Then Live?*)

D. M. Lloyd-Jones, *God the Father, God the Son*, London: Hodder & Stoughton, 1996.

D. M. Lloyd-Jones, *God the Holy Spirit*, London: Hodder & Stoughton, 1997.

D. M. Lloyd-Jones, *The Church & the Last Things*, London: Hodder & Stoughton, 1997 (Three volumes which uncover the essentials of the Christian faith)

A.M. Hodgkin, *Christ in all the Scriptures*, London: Marshall Pickering, 1989 (The testimony in each book of the Bible to Christ and their affirmation of him as the Son of God).

C.S. Lewis, *The Narnia Chronicles*, London: Harper Collins, 1950 et seq. (Seven allegorical tales for children of all ages).

C.S. Lewis, *The Screwtape Letters*, 1942 et seq Fount. (Letters from a retired elderly devil to a young devil who is learning the business of temptation).

O. Hallesby, *Prayer*, Leicester: IVP, 1948 ("The presentation of a few simple rules for the benefit of souls who are fainting in prayer").

Colin Webster *Time Well Spent* 1999 Alpha. (A practical guide to daily Quiet Times).

Os Guinness, *God in the Dark*, London:Hodder and Stoughton, 1996. (The dilemma of Doubt and how to resolve it.)

John Bunyan *The Pilgrim's Progress*, Oxford: OUP, 1998 ('An allegory from this world to that which is to come under the similitude of a dream').

Letters of Francis A. Schaeffer ed. Lane T. Dennis 1985: Crossway. (A collection of 97 of his letters chosen for their practical advice and spiritual insight.)

C.S. Lewis *Letters to Malcolm: Chiefly on Prayer* 1988, Fount. (Twenty-two letters to an imaginary correspondent on the subject of Prayer).

Jacques Ellul, *Reason for Being*, 1990 Eerdmans. (A meditation on Ecclesiastes).

Christopher Catherwood, *Martyn Lloyd-Jones: A Family Portrait* 1995:Kingswood. (Against the background of the preacher and the intellectual, the human side of 'the Doctor' is revealed).

A.M. Renwick & A.M. Harman, *The Story of the Church*, 1985, Leicester: IVP. (A concise summary of Christian history spanning twenty centuries).

B.F.C. Atkinson, *Valiant in Flight*, 1947 Leicester: IVP. (An account of God's dealings with his people in the past providing encouragement for present witness).

History of the Church 7 vols. 1990 London:Penguin. (Seven volumes by different scholars tracing the history of the Church.)

K. Birkett, *The Reformation* 1998, Matthias. (An account of the social and religious soil in which the Reformation grew, the events which shaped it and the ideas and doctrines for which many people died).

Os Guinness, *The Call* , 1998: Word. (Finding and fulfilling the central purpose of your life).

Neil Postman, *Amusing ourselves to Death*, 1987 et seq. Methuen. (Arguing that T.V. is transforming our culture into one vast arena for show business).

John White, *Money isn't God* 1993, Leicester: IVP. (So why is the church worshipping it? The author charges the western church with idolatry).

Brian Rosner, *How to get really rich*, 1999, Leicester: IVP. (A sharp exposé of what a greedy and materialistic lifestyle is doing to people, and to Christians).

Tony Payne and Phillip D. Jensen, *Pure Sex* Matthias Media 1998. (A book for all who are curious, or confused, dissatisfied, hurt or struggling with sexuality and who want some answers).

Nigel Pollock, *The Relationships Revolution*, 1998, Leicester: IVP (A clear Biblical worldview on Friendship, singleness and marriage).

Al Hsu, *The Single Issue*, 1997 Leicester: IVP (A splendid analysis and understanding of singleness).

Bill Hybels, *Christians in the Marketplace*, 1992, Victor Books (Making your faith work on the job).